IMAP: Modernizing Email Management

James Relington

DEDICATION

To those who seek knowledge, inspiration, and new perspectives—
may this book be a companion on your journey, a spark for curiosity,
and a reminder that every page turned is a step toward discovery.

One of the key strengths of IMAP within mobile environments is its inherent ability to provide real-time synchronization across multiple devices. IMAP maintains email data centrally on servers, meaning users who access their inbox through mobile devices always view the latest mailbox state. When actions such

AKNOWLEDGEMENTS

I would like to express my deepest gratitude to everyone who contributed to the creation of this book. To my colleagues and mentors, your insights and expertise have been invaluable. A special thank you to my family and friends for their unwavering support and encouragement throughout this journey.

Introduction to IMAP

Email management has evolved significantly since its inception, transitioning from simple message exchanges into an essential and complex communication ecosystem. Among the various protocols that facilitate this critical function, the Internet Message Access Protocol, commonly known as IMAP, has established itself as a cornerstone in modern email management practices. IMAP emerged primarily as an advanced alternative to earlier email retrieval protocols, such as POP3, which were somewhat restrictive in their capabilities. Unlike these early systems, IMAP is designed to synchronize email seamlessly across multiple devices, enabling users to manage and access their emails efficiently from different locations without data inconsistencies or duplication.

At its core, IMAP is an internet standard protocol used by email clients to retrieve email messages from a mail server. Its principal strength lies in its client-server architecture, allowing email messages to be stored centrally on a server and accessed dynamically from multiple clients. This represents a significant advantage for users who frequently switch devices or operate across various locations, ensuring that emails and their associated states—such as read, unread, flagged, or deleted—remain consistently updated. The robustness of IMAP in handling message statuses across numerous devices reflects a profound improvement over previous protocols that required downloading messages onto individual devices, creating a fragmented and often confusing email management experience.

IMAP's underlying structure emphasizes the synchronization of messages rather than simple retrieval, a nuance that underscores its modern relevance. When a user interacts with their email client—reading messages, deleting, marking as important, or moving emails between folders—these actions are immediately communicated back to the server. This interaction creates a synchronized environment where changes are instantly reflected on all connected devices. Such seamless synchronization is particularly valuable in today's interconnected world, where users expect real-time updates and consistent experiences, whether using smartphones, tablets, desktops, or web-based email interfaces.

The development of IMAP dates back several decades, originating from the need to address limitations inherent in earlier email protocols. POP3, the protocol widely used before IMAP, was designed primarily for offline use. Users were required to download their emails onto a single local machine, removing them from the server. Consequently, emails accessed from one device would not reflect accurately when accessed from another, resulting in disjointed email management. IMAP was introduced to overcome these significant drawbacks by ensuring that email data remained centrally located and synchronized across devices, thus fundamentally transforming email management into a more dynamic, accessible, and unified experience.

Another essential characteristic of IMAP that has enhanced its adoption is its advanced mailbox management capabilities. IMAP allows users to create, rename, delete, and organize mailboxes directly on the server, offering more extensive management possibilities than earlier protocols. This organizational capability means users can structure their email management in ways that best suit their workflows, preferences, or organizational requirements. Furthermore, IMAP supports hierarchical folders, enabling users to create complex and nested folder structures. The ability to manage and organize email efficiently has become increasingly important as email volumes grow, making IMAP's sophisticated mailbox management functionality critical to modern digital productivity.

Security also remains a foundational element of IMAP's relevance and broad adoption. Given the sensitive nature of much email communication—personal, corporate, financial, or otherwise confidential—securing email transmission and access has become paramount. IMAP inherently supports secure communications through SSL/TLS encryption, ensuring that emails and credentials are protected from interception or unauthorized access during transmission. Moreover, IMAP can be integrated with various authentication protocols, including modern methods such as OAuth2, further enhancing security by allowing secure authentication without relying solely on traditional username and password mechanisms.

IMAP's flexibility extends beyond personal email management, reaching into broader corporate and organizational environments. Enterprises frequently rely on IMAP for its ability to centralize email storage, facilitate compliance, and simplify backup procedures. Since emails remain on centralized servers, businesses can easily enforce retention policies, perform comprehensive backups, and conduct compliance audits with greater efficiency and accuracy. In complex environments where email data integrity and traceability are crucial, IMAP's centralized approach offers significant administrative advantages over older protocols that decentralized email storage.

Additionally, IMAP continues to evolve through extensions and enhancements that address the changing needs of digital communication. These extensions allow developers and service providers to introduce advanced functionalities, such as improved search capabilities, more efficient synchronization methods, and better resource management, continually modernizing and adapting IMAP to contemporary demands. As email continues to be one of the most ubiquitous forms of digital communication, such adaptability ensures that IMAP remains an essential protocol for both current and future email management strategies.

Today, IMAP stands as a testament to thoughtful technological advancement, offering users and administrators alike a robust, secure, and highly versatile email management solution. Its ability to synchronize email seamlessly across multiple devices, ensure data consistency, provide enhanced mailbox management, and facilitate strong security measures positions it as an indispensable tool in the modern digital landscape. Understanding IMAP, its functions, and its capabilities is foundational for anyone aiming to effectively manage digital communications in our interconnected age.

Understanding Email Protocols

Email is arguably one of the most influential innovations in digital communication, shaping the way individuals, businesses, and organizations exchange information globally. To fully grasp how email operates efficiently, reliably, and securely, it is crucial to understand the underlying protocols that enable email systems to function. These protocols define how messages are sent, received, managed, and stored across interconnected computer systems worldwide. Without these standardized methods, the seamless exchange of email across diverse platforms and devices would not be possible.

Email protocols are essentially sets of rules and procedures that facilitate communication between servers and clients in the transmission and retrieval of messages. They serve as a universal language that email servers and clients use to negotiate message transfer, authentication, and mailbox management. Several key protocols form the backbone of email communication, notably SMTP (Simple Mail Transfer Protocol), POP3 (Post Office Protocol Version 3), IMAP (Internet Message Access Protocol), and more recently, protocols that enhance email security and authentication, such as TLS (Transport Layer Security) and OAuth2. Each of these protocols addresses specific aspects of the email process, collectively contributing to the robust system users rely on daily.

SMTP is foundational in the process of sending emails. It defines how outgoing email messages are relayed between mail servers and eventually reach recipients' mailboxes. SMTP's primary responsibility is the secure and reliable transfer of messages across the internet, using standard TCP/IP communication. When an email is composed and sent, the sender's mail client initiates communication with an SMTP server, which then verifies the recipient's email address, routes the message through intermediate servers as necessary, and ensures its eventual delivery to the destination server. SMTP's design is inherently robust, featuring mechanisms for error reporting, retries, and delivery confirmation. Its role is critical because successful email communication fundamentally depends on accurate, timely, and secure message transmission between numerous interconnected systems.

While SMTP focuses on the sending of email, protocols such as POP3 and IMAP manage the retrieval of messages from email servers. POP3 was one of the earliest protocols introduced to allow email clients to fetch messages from servers and download them onto local devices. Designed in an era when internet connectivity was intermittent and slow, POP3 enabled users to download emails to their computers, allowing offline reading and storage. However, POP3 has notable limitations. Since messages typically reside on local devices rather than being synchronized across multiple systems, users often faced inconsistencies and duplication of messages when using multiple devices. Despite these limitations, POP3 remains useful in specific scenarios where offline storage is preferred, or internet connectivity is unreliable.

Recognizing the limitations of POP3, IMAP was developed as a more advanced and flexible protocol for retrieving and managing emails directly on mail servers. IMAP's approach differs significantly by emphasizing synchronization rather than one-time downloads. With IMAP, email messages are stored and managed centrally on servers, allowing real-time synchronization across multiple devices. When a user interacts with messages through one device—marking emails as read, deleting, or organizing them into folders—these actions instantly synchronize with the server and reflect across all connected devices. This synchronization capability positions IMAP as the preferred protocol for modern users who frequently access emails from smartphones, tablets, laptops, and desktop computers, providing a seamless and unified experience across multiple environments.

In addition to message transmission and retrieval, email protocols are increasingly focused on security and authentication, responding to growing threats such as spam, phishing, and data interception. Transport Layer Security (TLS) has become a fundamental component for securing email transmission, working alongside SMTP and IMAP to encrypt communications. TLS helps ensure emails and user credentials are transmitted securely across potentially insecure networks, significantly reducing vulnerabilities. Moreover, advanced authentication protocols such as OAuth2 are now commonly integrated into email systems to enhance security further. OAuth2 allows users to authenticate securely without directly sharing passwords, reducing risks associated with credential theft or compromise.

Understanding email protocols also involves acknowledging their interoperability and adaptability. Protocols are often extended or adapted to address evolving user demands and technological advancements. Email protocol extensions can add functionality, enhance performance, or bolster security without compromising the fundamental standards on which interoperability depends. These extensions enable email systems to remain responsive to contemporary needs, such as supporting large attachments, facilitating advanced search functions, or improving synchronization performance. The ongoing refinement of these protocols underscores the importance of maintaining compatibility and interoperability while ensuring that email systems remain effective and relevant in a rapidly evolving digital landscape.

Moreover, email protocols are designed to ensure compatibility across diverse platforms, email clients, and operating systems. The universal adoption of standardized protocols means that an email sent from one client—whether from a web browser, smartphone app, or desktop application—can be reliably received, interpreted, and displayed by another, regardless of technological differences. This universality is critical to email's global effectiveness, allowing for communication without requiring uniform software, hardware, or even network architecture among users.

Email protocols are the invisible foundation of modern digital communication, defining how billions of emails traverse the globe daily. Their robustness, security features, and continuous evolution ensure that email remains a dependable and secure channel for personal, commercial, and governmental communication. An in-depth understanding of these protocols helps clarify the complexities involved in seemingly straightforward email interactions, offering valuable insights into the technology underpinning one of the most fundamental communication methods in contemporary society.

The Evolution of IMAP

The Internet Message Access Protocol, known universally by its acronym IMAP, has undergone substantial evolution since its inception, transforming significantly to meet the demands of an increasingly connected digital environment. IMAP emerged initially as a direct response to the limitations inherent in earlier email retrieval protocols, particularly POP3, which dominated email communication throughout the early days of internet use. From its beginnings, IMAP sought to introduce flexibility, synchronization, and ease of access to email management, creating a robust framework that would enable seamless interaction across multiple devices and platforms. The journey of IMAP from its modest origins to the powerful and indispensable protocol it is today illustrates a broader story of technological advancement, user expectations, and the evolving nature of digital communication.

The earliest implementations of email management were straightforward, but severely limited in their flexibility. Initially, email protocols like POP3 provided the essential ability to retrieve emails from servers, but this was largely a unidirectional interaction. Users downloaded messages onto a single device, making subsequent synchronization across multiple devices difficult or impossible. This lack of synchronization created challenges, especially as computing habits evolved and users began accessing emails from different locations, often using more than one device to manage communications. Recognizing these limitations, Mark Crispin, working at Stanford University in the mid-1980s, introduced IMAP as

15

a more advanced alternative, with the goal of fundamentally changing the email experience by focusing heavily on synchronization and dynamic interaction between clients and servers.

The earliest version of IMAP, known initially as IMAP2, introduced basic functionalities that significantly enhanced email interaction compared to the static approach offered by POP3. IMAP2 allowed emails to be stored centrally on servers, ensuring that messages remained available and synchronized regardless of the number of devices accessing them. This centralization was revolutionary at the time, offering users a more consistent experience. The server-centric design meant users could read, manage, or delete messages without permanently affecting their ability to access them later from another location or device. IMAP2 effectively set the stage for a new era of flexible, user-friendly email management.

As the internet expanded dramatically through the 1990s, user needs and expectations continued to evolve rapidly. Email quickly became the primary form of professional and personal communication worldwide, prompting the introduction of IMAP3, which further enhanced the synchronization capabilities and introduced preliminary support for mailbox management. While IMAP3 was never officially standardized, it laid crucial groundwork for subsequent improvements. Its successor, IMAP4, officially standardized in the early 1990s, became the defining version of the protocol, incorporating comprehensive enhancements in mailbox management, folder hierarchies, advanced message handling, and richer synchronization features.

The IMAP4 specification represented a turning point, solidifying IMAP's position as a robust, scalable, and reliable email management protocol. With IMAP4, users gained unprecedented control over their email environments. The new specification provided advanced message flags, hierarchical folder structures, improved message searching capabilities, and sophisticated synchronization mechanisms, greatly expanding IMAP's appeal and utility. These features allowed users to categorize, organize, and retrieve email messages much more efficiently, adapting email usage to the more structured and productivity-focused digital workflows that businesses and organizations increasingly demanded.

As the digital landscape grew more complex in the late 1990s and early 2000s, security emerged as a critical concern for users and organizations alike. IMAP evolved in parallel, integrating support for encrypted connections via SSL and later TLS protocols. This advancement provided users greater confidence in their digital communications, ensuring messages and credentials transmitted between clients and servers remained secure against interception and unauthorized access. Furthermore, IMAP adapted readily to newer authentication standards, such as OAuth2, which allowed secure authentication methods without traditional reliance on passwords alone, significantly reducing risks associated with credential compromise or theft.

The growing ubiquity of mobile devices and smartphones throughout the early 2000s further emphasized IMAP's importance and versatility. Mobile users required seamless, real-time synchronization and efficient management of their email, regardless of location or device type. IMAP's server-based synchronization perfectly addressed these demands, supporting instant updates of message status across multiple mobile devices, a feature that rapidly became indispensable. As mobile computing became commonplace, IMAP continued adapting and optimizing its synchronization mechanisms, improving performance and efficiency even on bandwidth-constrained mobile networks.

Throughout its evolution, IMAP's extensibility proved critical to its enduring relevance. IMAP's modular nature allowed extensions and modifications without compromising compatibility or interoperability. This adaptability meant that the protocol could easily incorporate new functionalities to address emerging needs. Extensions allowed IMAP servers and clients to handle modern features such as push notifications (IMAP IDLE), compressed data exchanges, improved searching, and sophisticated filtering mechanisms, ensuring that IMAP continued adapting to contemporary communication demands.

In recent years, IMAP continues its evolution, increasingly integrating with cloud-based and hybrid email environments. As email management shifts toward cloud storage and services, IMAP's centralized server approach naturally aligns with contemporary cloud computing models. Organizations find IMAP advantageous because emails remain centrally stored and managed, simplifying compliance with data retention policies, enabling more straightforward backup strategies, and supporting effective disaster recovery plans.

The evolution of IMAP reflects broader trends within technology and digital communication, where adaptability, synchronization, and security define user expectations. Each iteration of IMAP has responded directly to changing user requirements, technological advancements, and emerging security threats. The ongoing development of IMAP ensures its continued relevance and positions it as an essential component of the modern digital communication ecosystem, reliably serving billions of users worldwide.

IMAP vs. POP3: A Comparison

When exploring email management systems, two critical protocols inevitably become central to the discussion: IMAP (Internet Message Access Protocol) and POP3 (Post Office Protocol version 3). Each has played a significant role in the history of email communications, yet they differ profoundly in functionality, usability, and practical implementation. Understanding the distinctions between IMAP and POP3 is essential for both casual users and administrators aiming to select an appropriate protocol for their email management needs. The comparison between these protocols reveals fundamental differences in how emails are accessed, managed, and stored, profoundly impacting user experiences, especially in today's increasingly interconnected digital environment.

POP3 was developed initially during the era when internet access was intermittent, bandwidth was limited, and users typically accessed email from a single, stationary device, such as a personal computer at home or at work. As a result, POP3 was designed around simplicity, efficiency, and the basic concept of retrieving emails from a remote server and downloading them locally onto the user's computer. Once downloaded, the emails were typically removed from the server, leaving the only copy stored locally on the user's device. While this approach served early internet users efficiently, it eventually created significant limitations in terms of accessibility and synchronization across multiple devices. Users who accessed emails from different devices or locations found themselves encountering discrepancies, with emails appearing unread or absent on some devices but not others, as POP3 could not inherently synchronize message states.

In contrast, IMAP was explicitly designed to overcome these limitations. Instead of downloading and deleting messages from the server, IMAP maintains email messages centrally stored on the mail server. This centralization provides continuous and synchronized access to emails, ensuring users always have consistent visibility and management across all their connected devices, whether using a smartphone, tablet, laptop, or desktop computer. The core advantage of IMAP is precisely this synchronization capability: any action performed on one device—such as reading, deleting, flagging, or organizing emails—is immediately reflected across all connected clients, creating a uniform and cohesive user experience.

Additionally, the differing storage approaches between IMAP and POP3 have significant implications. Since POP3 downloads and stores messages locally, storage requirements and management responsibilities fall primarily onto users' individual devices. If the device fails, experiences hardware issues, or becomes compromised, users risk losing their entire email history unless proactive backups are regularly performed. Conversely, IMAP's server-based approach inherently simplifies backups, as emails remain stored centrally, typically benefiting from automated, routine server-level backups managed by service providers or organizational IT departments. Thus, IMAP significantly reduces the risk of email loss associated with hardware failure or device replacement.

Beyond storage and synchronization, IMAP and POP3 differ considerably in terms of mailbox management capabilities. POP3 has minimal built-in mailbox management functionality, primarily allowing users only to retrieve messages sequentially. It does not inherently support advanced features such as hierarchical folder structures or real-time email organization on the server. Consequently, mailbox organization under POP3 occurs only on the user's local device, limiting flexibility and potentially leading to confusion and inefficiency when managing large volumes of email. IMAP, in contrast, offers robust and extensive mailbox management features directly on the mail server. Users can create, delete, rename, and manage multiple folders and subfolders remotely, greatly enhancing organizational flexibility. This capability is especially beneficial for users and organizations that manage substantial email volumes and need complex folder structures for clarity, organization, and compliance purposes.

Security represents another significant area of distinction between IMAP and POP3. Although both protocols can utilize secure encryption protocols such as SSL/TLS for secure message transmission, IMAP's ongoing development and adaptability have enabled more sophisticated security enhancements and authentication methods, such as OAuth2. OAuth2 significantly improves authentication security by reducing reliance on direct password exchanges, a crucial advantage given today's cybersecurity threats. POP3, while still supporting encryption, often lags behind IMAP regarding modern security enhancements, partly due to its simpler, older architecture, and because contemporary email services frequently prioritize IMAP development to address evolving security threats.

Performance and bandwidth usage also differentiate the two protocols. POP3 typically requires users to download entire messages, including large attachments, before reading them. This approach can lead to delays, particularly on slower connections or when managing emails with extensive attachments. On the other hand, IMAP allows users to preview email headers or selectively download portions of messages, improving performance by reducing bandwidth consumption. This selective retrieval capability significantly enhances usability, especially in scenarios with limited bandwidth, such as mobile data networks or remote locations.

User behavior and expectations have evolved dramatically since the inception of both protocols. Today's email users demand instantaneous access, continuous synchronization, secure handling, and efficient mailbox management capabilities—qualities that inherently align more closely with IMAP than POP3. Nevertheless, POP3 still maintains relevance in specific scenarios, particularly where offline access to emails is essential, or internet connectivity remains unreliable or expensive. For users or organizations with straightforward, singular-device setups or limited connectivity, POP3 remains a practical, if limited, solution.

Overall, the comparison between IMAP and POP3 illustrates the evolution of email protocols, reflecting broader shifts in user expectations and technological environments. While POP3 originated in an era of simpler, stationary computing needs, IMAP aligns closely with contemporary expectations for seamless, secure, and synchronized digital communication. As email continues to serve as a foundational communication tool, understanding these distinctions enables users and administrators to choose protocols that best match their specific requirements, thereby optimizing email management and overall digital productivity.

Architecture of IMAP Servers

The architecture of IMAP servers is designed to support robust, flexible, and efficient email management across multiple devices and platforms, a necessity driven by the increasing complexity and scale of contemporary digital communication. IMAP servers utilize a sophisticated client-server model, carefully structured to manage email storage, retrieval, synchronization, and security effectively. The design principles guiding IMAP architecture prioritize accessibility, consistency, and scalability, ensuring the protocol meets the diverse needs of individual users, enterprises, and large-scale service providers.

At the core of IMAP server architecture lies the fundamental concept of centralized mail storage. Unlike protocols such as POP3, which transfer emails from the server directly onto individual client devices, IMAP maintains email messages centrally stored on the server itself. This central storage model ensures that users can access their messages consistently from multiple locations and various devices without experiencing synchronization issues or inconsistencies. Emails remain safely and reliably stored on the server until explicitly deleted by the user, providing considerable advantages for email management, data integrity, and recovery. Centralized storage also significantly simplifies administrative tasks such as backups, compliance management, and disaster recovery planning, reducing complexity and administrative overhead for organizations.

IMAP servers typically consist of multiple logical layers working together seamlessly to ensure optimal performance, reliability, and security. The uppermost layer is the IMAP protocol handler, which manages direct communication with email clients. When a client application initiates a connection to the IMAP server, this protocol handler processes authentication requests, manages user sessions, and facilitates commands related to mailbox operations such as message retrieval, status updates, searching, and folder management. By managing these functions, the IMAP protocol handler ensures that client interactions remain responsive, secure, and efficient.

Beneath the protocol handler lies the mailbox management layer, responsible for organizing and maintaining emails stored on the server. This layer handles the creation, deletion, renaming, and organization of mailboxes and folders, managing complex hierarchical structures that allow users to categorize and store messages systematically. The mailbox management layer also keeps track of message metadata, such as read and unread status, flags indicating importance or follow-up tasks, and timestamps, ensuring that synchronization across devices remains accurate. It is this layer that enables sophisticated mailbox manipulation, providing users with extensive control over their email environments and significantly enhancing productivity by allowing efficient retrieval and management of stored messages.

Another critical component in IMAP server architecture is the data storage layer, where emails and associated attachments are physically stored. This layer typically utilizes advanced database systems or specialized file-based storage structures optimized to handle large volumes of data efficiently. Given that email servers can store thousands or even millions of messages, scalability and reliability become paramount in storage design. High-performance databases or optimized file systems ensure rapid message retrieval, efficient searching and indexing, and effective handling of attachments and large data objects. Additionally, this layer must ensure robust data integrity, implementing techniques such as redundancy, replication, and backup strategies to protect against data loss, corruption, or server failures.

IMAP servers also incorporate robust security mechanisms at multiple architectural levels. Security begins with authentication and access control, where users must verify their identities before accessing mailboxes or performing mailbox operations. IMAP supports various authentication methods, including traditional username/password schemes and modern, secure authentication protocols like OAuth2. Once authenticated, communication between clients and IMAP servers typically leverages SSL/TLS encryption to secure data transmitted over the network, ensuring confidentiality and protecting sensitive information against interception or unauthorized access. Furthermore, IMAP servers integrate security practices such as intrusion detection systems, logging mechanisms, and real-time monitoring to proactively identify, prevent, or respond to security threats.

Scalability is another crucial aspect of IMAP server architecture. Modern IMAP systems are designed to handle large numbers of simultaneous connections, manage extensive mailbox sizes, and efficiently serve thousands of users concurrently. To achieve this scalability, IMAP servers employ strategies such as load balancing, clustering, and distributed storage. Load balancing distributes incoming connections evenly across multiple server nodes, preventing performance bottlenecks or service degradation during periods of high usage. Clustering allows servers to operate in coordinated groups, providing redundancy and high availability, enabling continuous service even if individual servers experience failure or require maintenance. Distributed storage solutions further enhance scalability, allowing email data to reside across multiple storage nodes, significantly enhancing performance, redundancy, and reliability.

Integration capabilities represent an additional dimension of IMAP server architecture, as IMAP servers frequently interface with other email-related systems and services. IMAP servers often integrate with SMTP servers to manage outbound messages seamlessly. Additionally, integration with directory services such as LDAP enables centralized user management, simplifying administration tasks such as provisioning, account management, and security policies. Modern IMAP servers may also integrate with email filtering systems, spam prevention services, archival solutions, and compliance management tools, forming a comprehensive ecosystem that streamlines email operations and enhances overall organizational efficiency.

The architecture of IMAP servers continues to evolve in response to changing user demands, technological advancements, and emerging threats. As email volumes grow, IMAP server architectures increasingly leverage cloud-based infrastructures and virtualization technologies, enabling dynamic scaling of resources, rapid deployment, and simplified administration. Innovations such as containerization and microservices architectures further enhance IMAP server efficiency, flexibility, and scalability, positioning IMAP for continued relevance in managing the vast digital communication flows characteristic of today's interconnected world.

Client-Server Communication in IMAP

Client-server communication is central to the functionality of the Internet Message Access Protocol (IMAP), forming the essential foundation upon which modern email synchronization and retrieval operate. The fundamental design of IMAP centers on a continuous and interactive dialogue between client applications, such as email software running on personal computers or mobile devices, and the IMAP server, where email messages and associated data are stored. The effectiveness, reliability, and robustness of email management significantly depend upon the precise, consistent, and secure communication between these two components, making client-server interactions within IMAP a subject of critical importance for users, administrators, and developers alike.

At its most basic level, IMAP client-server communication begins when a user's email client initiates a connection to the IMAP server. This initial connection typically occurs over TCP/IP network channels, using standardized network ports specifically assigned to IMAP communications. Once established, this connection serves as a persistent channel through which all subsequent interactions occur, ensuring consistent synchronization and real-time responsiveness. Persistence of the connection, as opposed to intermittent communication, distinguishes IMAP significantly from simpler protocols such as POP3, facilitating real-time updates and seamless synchronization across multiple client devices. Persistent connections also improve performance by eliminating repeated reconnections, which consume resources and introduce latency into email retrieval operations.

When an IMAP client establishes a connection with the server, authentication represents the immediate and critical first step of their interaction. Secure and reliable authentication procedures ensure that access to email data is restricted only to authorized users. IMAP supports multiple authentication methods, including traditional username and password schemes as well as more advanced approaches like OAuth2. OAuth2 authentication provides enhanced security by issuing tokens that grant clients access without directly exchanging passwords. Following successful authentication, the IMAP server maintains an authenticated session, during which the client can perform operations such as message retrieval, mailbox management, message searching, and synchronization actions.

Once authenticated, IMAP client-server communication typically involves the exchange of commands and responses structured according to a clearly defined protocol syntax. Each action the client intends to perform—such as retrieving messages, moving emails between folders, or updating message flags—initiates a structured command sent from the client to the IMAP server. These commands are textual, precisely formatted instructions indicating specific requests or operations. The server processes these commands, executing the requested actions, and subsequently sends structured responses back to the client, confirming completion, providing requested data, or indicating any errors or exceptions encountered during processing. This back-and-forth exchange occurs rapidly, enabling immediate feedback and ensuring that client-side actions promptly synchronize with the central email store on the server.

The interactive and structured nature of IMAP communication also enables more sophisticated mailbox operations compared to earlier, simpler email protocols. Through clearly defined commands, IMAP allows clients to manage complex mailbox structures directly on the server. Users can create, rename, or delete mailboxes; organize messages into hierarchical folders; search messages based on complex criteria; and manipulate message status flags indicating attributes such as read/unread, important, or deleted. These operations occur transparently on the server side, immediately reflecting on all client devices connected to the IMAP account. Such server-side management significantly enhances the user experience, providing users with extensive control over their email organization and retrieval processes.

The efficiency and responsiveness of IMAP communication are enhanced by specific protocol mechanisms designed to optimize client-server interactions. For instance, IMAP supports the IDLE command, a critical enhancement that enables push-based email notifications. Using the IDLE command, the client remains connected passively, waiting for the server to send immediate notifications about new emails or mailbox status changes without requiring active polling from the client. This push mechanism significantly reduces bandwidth consumption, improves efficiency, and provides users with instantaneous updates about new messages or mailbox changes. Consequently, IMAP IDLE has become essential, especially in mobile email management scenarios, where resource efficiency and timely notifications are paramount.

Security remains a critical consideration throughout the IMAP client-server communication process. IMAP inherently supports encryption protocols such as SSL/TLS, ensuring that the data transmitted between clients and servers remains confidential and protected against interception or unauthorized access. Encrypted IMAP connections are standard practice, especially in corporate and organizational environments where sensitive or proprietary information regularly traverses email systems. This secure transmission capability reassures users that their private communications and credentials remain secure during the entire client-server interaction.

Performance considerations further shape IMAP client-server interactions, particularly in scenarios involving limited bandwidth or high network latency. IMAP protocol commands permit selective retrieval of message content, enabling clients to fetch only message headers or partial content rather than entire messages and attachments. By selectively retrieving only essential data, clients significantly improve email responsiveness and reduce bandwidth consumption, enhancing user experience in low-bandwidth environments or mobile networks. These selective retrieval capabilities illustrate IMAP's adaptability, highlighting its design responsiveness to the diverse and evolving technological environments in which users now manage their digital communications.

Scalability represents another important dimension of IMAP client-server communication. Modern IMAP servers are engineered to manage thousands or even millions of simultaneous connections, ensuring consistent performance and responsiveness across large-scale deployments. Scalability is achieved through architectural strategies such as load balancing, clustering, and distributed storage, ensuring that the IMAP server infrastructure efficiently manages substantial concurrent communications without degradation of performance. The robustness of IMAP's client-server communication design allows it to meet the demanding expectations of large organizations and service providers, facilitating smooth and consistent email management experiences for diverse user populations.

IMAP's client-server communication model effectively addresses the complexities and demands of contemporary digital communication, offering users seamless, secure, and efficient email synchronization and management. The structured, interactive nature of this communication, combined with its emphasis on real-time synchronization, robust security, scalability, and efficient resource usage, positions IMAP as an indispensable component of modern email infrastructure.

Securing IMAP Communications

Securing IMAP communications is a critical element in managing email effectively in today's digitally interconnected environment. IMAP (Internet Message Access Protocol) serves as a key protocol facilitating the synchronization and management of email across multiple devices, yet the inherent openness of internet-based communication channels creates significant security risks. Ensuring the privacy, integrity, and confidentiality of email data transmitted via IMAP requires comprehensive strategies and robust implementations to protect sensitive information against unauthorized access, interception, manipulation, or theft.

At its core, IMAP operates through continuous interactions between email clients and servers over networks, frequently the internet. Without appropriate security measures, these interactions could expose users' emails, attachments, and credentials to significant vulnerabilities. To mitigate such risks, IMAP incorporates strong security mechanisms, primarily through encrypted communications utilizing SSL/TLS protocols. These encryption methods form the backbone of secure IMAP interactions, protecting transmitted data from interception by unauthorized third parties. SSL (Secure Sockets Layer), historically employed for secure email communication, has largely been replaced by the more secure and reliable TLS (Transport Layer Security). TLS provides robust encryption, ensuring that all data exchanged between IMAP clients and servers is securely encrypted during transmission, making it unreadable to anyone attempting interception without proper cryptographic keys.

TLS encryption in IMAP operates by establishing a secure communication channel before email data transmission begins. Initially, the client and server perform a secure handshake, exchanging cryptographic keys to authenticate each party's identity. This handshake confirms that the server is legitimate and ensures both parties use a secure cipher suite for the encrypted communication. Once established, this encrypted tunnel ensures that data remains confidential throughout the session. Using strong encryption standards, such as TLS 1.2 or TLS 1.3, IMAP servers ensure robust protection against emerging threats, vulnerabilities, and exploits, offering significantly enhanced security compared to older, less secure protocols.

Authentication represents another critical aspect of securing IMAP communications. Properly validating the identity of users accessing IMAP servers is essential for preventing unauthorized access and protecting sensitive email data. Traditional IMAP authentication relied on simple username and password mechanisms, which posed significant risks due to potential password interception or theft. To overcome these vulnerabilities, modern IMAP implementations incorporate advanced authentication methods, including OAuth2 and multi-factor authentication (MFA). OAuth2 provides a highly secure method of authentication by issuing time-limited access tokens, reducing reliance on directly transmitting or storing passwords. With

OAuth2, users authenticate once through secure identity providers, granting the IMAP client temporary access to their email accounts without repeated password exchanges, thus significantly minimizing credential exposure.

Multi-factor authentication further strengthens IMAP security by requiring users to verify their identities through additional authentication layers beyond traditional passwords. MFA may involve combinations of something the user knows, such as a password, something they have, such as a mobile device generating temporary codes, or biometric verification like fingerprints or facial recognition. Implementing MFA alongside OAuth2 significantly enhances IMAP authentication security, providing substantial protection against common cyber threats such as phishing, credential theft, and brute-force attacks.

IMAP security extends beyond authentication and encryption, encompassing strategies for secure mailbox storage, management, and access control. Secure mailbox storage involves implementing robust server-side measures to protect email messages stored centrally on IMAP servers. These measures typically include file-level encryption, access control lists (ACLs), and strong permissions management. File-level encryption ensures that email data remains encrypted even at rest on the server, reducing risks associated with unauthorized physical or remote server access. ACLs enable administrators to define precise access permissions for individual users or groups, ensuring users have only the appropriate access levels to mailboxes, folders, and message contents, thereby limiting potential exposure or misuse.

Moreover, IMAP security encompasses protecting email servers themselves against cyber threats, including intrusion attempts, malware infections, denial-of-service attacks, and other malicious activities. Securing IMAP servers requires implementing robust firewalls, intrusion detection and prevention systems (IDS/IPS), and real-time monitoring and logging tools. Firewalls provide essential perimeter defense, restricting unauthorized access attempts and protecting IMAP servers from external threats. IDS/IPS solutions proactively monitor network traffic, identify suspicious activities or unauthorized attempts to access IMAP services, and respond immediately to mitigate potential breaches or threats.

Regular monitoring and logging of IMAP communications further enhance security, providing comprehensive visibility into activities occurring on email servers. Logs capturing detailed information about authentication attempts, mailbox access, configuration changes, and failed login attempts enable administrators to detect abnormal patterns or unauthorized access attempts proactively. Such logging facilitates rapid identification, investigation, and response to potential security incidents, significantly reducing risks and strengthening overall email system security.

Maintaining up-to-date IMAP server software and applying security patches regularly is another crucial element in securing IMAP communications. Email servers, like all software systems, periodically discover vulnerabilities, which attackers may exploit. Timely updates and patches from IMAP software vendors ensure that servers maintain defenses against known vulnerabilities, significantly reducing potential attack surfaces and enhancing security posture.

End-user education represents another vital component of securing IMAP communications, as many email-related threats exploit user vulnerabilities or behaviors. Educating users about risks such as phishing, suspicious attachments, password security, and the importance of secure authentication practices significantly enhances overall security by reducing human-related vulnerabilities. Users who understand and adhere to recommended security practices provide an additional protective layer, complementing technical security measures implemented on IMAP servers.

As the cyber threat landscape continues to evolve rapidly, securing IMAP communications requires ongoing vigilance, proactive strategies, and comprehensive implementations. Organizations must continuously assess security risks, regularly update encryption standards, monitor authentication methods, and ensure end-to-end protection from client devices to IMAP servers. Through robust encryption, advanced authentication, comprehensive monitoring, proactive threat prevention, continuous software updates, and user education, IMAP communications can achieve the high levels of security essential for protecting today's critical digital communication channels.

Authentication Methods for IMAP

Authentication methods for IMAP (Internet Message Access Protocol) play a crucial role in ensuring secure and reliable access to email communications. As IMAP facilitates email synchronization and retrieval across multiple devices and networks, robust authentication practices become essential in protecting sensitive information from unauthorized access or cyber threats. Effective authentication ensures that only legitimate users can access mailboxes, safeguarding data integrity and user privacy, and preventing potential misuse of email accounts.

Initially, IMAP servers relied primarily on simple username and password mechanisms for user authentication. While this traditional method remains widespread, it presents significant vulnerabilities. Password-based authentication depends entirely on the confidentiality of the user's credentials, which can be compromised through phishing attacks, data breaches, or intercepted network transmissions. Even when encrypted, passwords may still be vulnerable to guessing or brute-force attacks, especially if users select weak or predictable passwords. Additionally, repeated transmission of passwords between IMAP clients and servers can increase the risk of exposure, particularly if secure encryption methods are inadequately configured or improperly implemented.

To address these inherent weaknesses, IMAP authentication has evolved significantly, incorporating more secure and advanced methods designed to reduce dependency on password exchanges and enhance overall security. One prominent solution that has emerged is OAuth2, a modern authentication protocol widely adopted by major email service providers. OAuth2 fundamentally transforms the authentication process by issuing access tokens instead of transmitting user credentials directly between clients and servers. When using OAuth2 with IMAP, the user authenticates once through a trusted identity provider, such as Google or Microsoft. After successful authentication, the identity provider issues a limited-duration access token that grants the IMAP client permission to access email resources without repeatedly exchanging passwords. This significantly reduces credential exposure risks and prevents unauthorized reuse of passwords.

OAuth2 provides considerable advantages beyond security alone. It allows for granular control of access privileges, enabling administrators and users to define precisely which IMAP client operations are permitted. Access tokens can be limited by time or scope, meaning they automatically expire or become invalid if unauthorized attempts are detected. Such controlled access mechanisms ensure that even if tokens are compromised, potential damage remains minimal. The adoption of OAuth2 in IMAP environments reflects broader shifts in authentication practices toward minimizing reliance on passwords and adopting stronger, token-based methods.

Another critical authentication advancement for IMAP is the widespread adoption of Multi-factor Authentication (MFA), also known as Two-factor Authentication (2FA). MFA significantly enhances authentication security by requiring users to verify their identity through multiple independent verification factors. Typically, MFA combines something the user knows, such as a password, with something the user possesses, like a smartphone app generating temporary access codes, or biometric verification methods, such as fingerprint scans or facial recognition. Requiring multiple verification factors dramatically reduces the risk of unauthorized account access, even if passwords become compromised, as attackers would need physical possession of a secondary authentication factor or biometric identification.

Implementing MFA in IMAP environments can pose technical challenges due to compatibility issues or legacy client limitations. To address these challenges, service providers often employ application-specific passwords or dedicated access codes generated explicitly for IMAP clients incapable of directly supporting MFA protocols. While application-specific passwords introduce complexity, they substantially improve security by preventing attackers from using compromised credentials for unauthorized account access. Overcoming compatibility challenges associated with MFA implementation remains crucial for IMAP administrators committed to enhancing authentication security.

An additional secure authentication method used in IMAP is client-side certificate authentication. Certificate-based authentication provides robust security by requiring client devices to present digital certificates, issued by trusted authorities, during the authentication process. Digital certificates contain cryptographic keys verifying the identity of the client device attempting IMAP access. This method offers several security advantages, notably the elimination of passwords altogether, reducing credential management burdens, and significantly enhancing resistance against phishing attacks. However, certificate-based authentication requires careful management and administration, including secure certificate provisioning, renewal processes, and revocation management.

Furthermore, IMAP authentication increasingly leverages directory-based identity management solutions, such as LDAP (Lightweight Directory Access Protocol), especially within organizational or enterprise environments. LDAP integration allows IMAP servers to authenticate users against centralized identity databases, providing consistent authentication management across multiple systems and applications. Centralized authentication simplifies administration tasks, including user provisioning, password management, and policy enforcement, significantly enhancing overall security. Moreover, centralized directory authentication aligns closely with organizational security policies, enabling administrators to enforce consistent password complexity requirements, periodic password rotations, and access control standards uniformly across the enterprise environment.

Authentication methods in IMAP are continuously evolving in response to emerging threats, user demands, and technological advancements. Innovations in biometric authentication, secure hardware tokens, and cryptographic standards regularly influence IMAP authentication strategies, further enhancing security capabilities. IMAP server providers and administrators remain proactive, consistently monitoring cybersecurity developments and integrating new, more secure authentication techniques to protect sensitive email data comprehensively.

Effective authentication also depends on user education and awareness. Educating users regarding the importance of selecting secure passwords, recognizing phishing attempts, and responsibly managing credentials significantly enhances overall authentication security. Well-informed users contribute positively toward securing email systems, complementing technological measures implemented within IMAP authentication processes.

Authentication methods for IMAP form an essential foundation for secure, efficient, and reliable email management. While traditional password authentication remains common, the introduction and adoption of advanced authentication methods such as OAuth2, multi-factor authentication, certificate-based methods, and centralized directory integration significantly enhance security capabilities, reducing vulnerabilities associated with credential theft or unauthorized access. Continued advancement and careful implementation of authentication protocols ensure that IMAP remains resilient against emerging cybersecurity threats, maintaining trust and reliability essential for effective digital communication.

IMAP Mailbox Management

Effective mailbox management is one of the defining characteristics of IMAP (Internet Message Access Protocol), providing users with powerful capabilities to organize, maintain, and manipulate email messages directly on the server. Unlike previous email protocols, IMAP places significant emphasis on server-side storage and management, enabling sophisticated email organization and dynamic access across multiple client devices. As digital communication continues to grow exponentially, efficient mailbox management has become increasingly crucial, ensuring users can easily access, locate, and manage vast volumes of email messages without experiencing clutter, confusion, or inefficiency.

Central to IMAP mailbox management is the concept of hierarchical folder structures, which significantly differentiates IMAP from earlier email protocols. IMAP allows users to create, organize, and maintain folders and subfolders directly on the mail server, enabling the logical categorization and storage of email messages according to users' individual or organizational needs. The ability to structure mailboxes hierarchically provides significant benefits, allowing users to group messages by subject, sender, date, or priority, thereby enhancing productivity and simplifying retrieval processes. Users can readily move messages between folders, rename folders, or delete entire folders without affecting their access from any other connected devices, ensuring consistency and synchronization across various email clients.

IMAP mailbox management also supports advanced features for message organization and classification, utilizing a range of standardized flags and attributes. These message attributes include marking messages as read or unread, flagging important or urgent emails, identifying messages for follow-up tasks, and marking items as deleted or archived. The implementation of these attributes provides immediate visual cues to users, enabling them to quickly assess message status, prioritize tasks, and manage workflow effectively. These flags are synchronized across all client devices through IMAP servers, ensuring consistency and visibility regardless of how many devices a user employs to access their mailbox.

Efficient mailbox management under IMAP also relies on advanced search capabilities. IMAP servers allow sophisticated searching directly on the server, enabling users to locate specific messages efficiently based on multiple criteria, including sender addresses, recipients, keywords in message subjects or bodies, attachments, message dates, and various flag statuses. Server-side searching significantly enhances productivity, particularly in large-scale mailboxes containing thousands of messages, reducing the need for manual sorting or scrolling through extensive message lists. By conducting complex searches directly on the IMAP server, users can rapidly identify and access relevant email content without excessive delay or frustration.

Storage efficiency is another critical aspect of IMAP mailbox management. IMAP's centralized storage model means that mailbox quotas and storage management become essential considerations, particularly in organizational or enterprise environments. Administrators often implement mailbox size quotas, ensuring individual users do not exceed designated storage limits, thereby optimizing overall server resources and performance. Effective mailbox management thus involves routine maintenance tasks such as archiving old or infrequently accessed messages, deleting unnecessary or duplicate emails, and regularly reviewing mailbox content. Users and administrators alike frequently leverage automated mailbox management tools and scripts integrated with IMAP servers, assisting in storage optimization and routine housekeeping tasks.

Compliance and data retention requirements significantly influence mailbox management practices in organizational contexts. Enterprises often need to adhere to regulatory mandates dictating specific email retention periods or compliance standards for legal purposes. IMAP's centralized management capabilities facilitate compliance by allowing administrators to enforce consistent retention policies across user mailboxes. Server-side retention rules can automatically archive or purge emails based on defined periods, subjects, senders, or other specific criteria, ensuring consistent adherence to compliance requirements while minimizing administrative overhead.

Security and privacy considerations also shape IMAP mailbox management strategies. Administrators routinely implement access controls, defining user permissions regarding mailbox viewing, editing, deleting, or moving messages within folders. IMAP servers frequently integrate access control lists (ACLs), enabling fine-grained permission management and restricting mailbox access based on defined roles or user groups. Properly configured access controls ensure that mailbox content remains accessible only to authorized individuals, safeguarding sensitive information and enhancing overall security.

Backup and recovery processes represent an integral component of effective IMAP mailbox management, ensuring protection against data loss, corruption, or accidental deletions. Due to IMAP's centralized storage model, regular backups of server-stored email data simplify disaster recovery, allowing administrators to restore mailboxes or individual messages quickly if required. Backups can be automated through server-level backup systems, capturing incremental changes periodically or performing full mailbox backups according to defined schedules. Robust backup procedures significantly enhance the resilience of email systems, ensuring continued availability and rapid recovery in the event of technical issues or cybersecurity incidents.

Performance considerations also influence IMAP mailbox management practices. Large mailboxes containing tens of thousands of messages can degrade client performance, causing slow synchronization or retrieval delays. To mitigate performance issues, mailbox management strategies often incorporate regular mailbox maintenance, message indexing, folder optimization, and performance monitoring. Administrators frequently implement mailbox indexing solutions to enhance retrieval speeds and reduce latency when searching or accessing messages, significantly improving user experience. Performance monitoring ensures that mailbox storage remains balanced across server resources, proactively identifying and resolving performance bottlenecks or storage inefficiencies.

Automation technologies increasingly support IMAP mailbox management tasks, especially in large-scale or enterprise environments. Server-side scripts, intelligent rules, and mailbox management tools automate routine tasks such as message filtering, categorization, and archiving. Automation enables users to establish rules that automatically sort incoming messages, flag urgent emails, move messages to designated folders, or perform periodic mailbox cleanup. This reduces manual effort and enhances productivity, allowing users to focus on priority tasks rather than managing email clutter continuously.

As digital communication volumes grow continuously, IMAP mailbox management remains a critical aspect of effective email communication. Hierarchical folder management, advanced message classification features, robust search capabilities, storage efficiency, compliance adherence, security controls, robust backup strategies, performance optimization, and automation collectively enable users and organizations to manage large-scale email effectively, ensuring productivity, security, and reliability across diverse digital environments.

Folder Hierarchies and Organization

Folder hierarchies and organization represent a core component of effective email management within IMAP (Internet Message Access Protocol), significantly enhancing users' ability to systematically store, access, and manage emails. With the increasing volume and complexity of digital communications, users face the challenge of keeping their email environments organized and efficient. IMAP addresses this challenge directly by enabling advanced, hierarchical folder structures stored centrally on servers, thereby ensuring that email management remains consistent and synchronized across multiple client devices.

The hierarchical organization of folders in IMAP systems facilitates logical categorization, enabling users to structure their mailboxes intuitively and flexibly. Unlike earlier email protocols, which provided limited or no capability for creating nested folders, IMAP permits users to construct elaborate folder structures, creating subfolders within folders as deeply nested as necessary. This organizational capability dramatically improves email handling, allowing users to categorize messages effectively by subject matter, sender, importance, project, or any other user-defined criteria. Hierarchical structures also make navigating large email repositories more intuitive, reducing the time required to locate messages and improving overall productivity.

Folder hierarchies in IMAP are not merely visual or superficial; they are directly managed and maintained on the email server itself. This server-side management ensures that the hierarchy is consistent and accessible across all connected clients, regardless of whether users access email through desktop applications, mobile devices, or web-based interfaces. Whenever users create, rename, or delete folders within an IMAP account, these actions immediately reflect on the server, synchronizing instantly to all other devices accessing the mailbox. This synchronization ensures uniformity in mailbox organization, significantly reducing user frustration and confusion associated with inconsistencies arising from managing multiple client applications.

Effective folder organization through IMAP also enhances users' ability to manage workflows, track project-related communications, and prioritize tasks efficiently. Users can establish specialized folders for specific projects, clients, or tasks, quickly grouping related messages together. These folders can further include nested subfolders for tasks completed, pending actions, or critical updates. By maintaining clear and logical folder structures, users ensure that essential communications are always readily accessible, significantly streamlining their workflow and enhancing productivity.

Moreover, hierarchical folder management within IMAP provides substantial benefits for managing large volumes of email messages. As email traffic increases, cluttered inboxes can become overwhelming, negatively impacting users' productivity and responsiveness. IMAP's structured folder approach allows users to move less critical or archived messages away from primary inboxes into designated folders. This decluttering effect significantly reduces cognitive load, helping users maintain focus on immediate or priority messages. Organizing emails systematically into folders and subfolders not only optimizes storage efficiency but also accelerates message retrieval, making even large-scale mailboxes manageable and efficient.

IMAP's robust folder hierarchy support extends to advanced mailbox operations, including searching, filtering, and rule-based automation. Users can leverage IMAP-compatible email clients to define rules or filters that automatically route incoming emails into appropriate folders based on specified criteria such as sender, keywords, dates, or subject lines. These automated rules dramatically enhance mailbox efficiency by systematically categorizing messages upon arrival, eliminating repetitive manual sorting tasks, and reducing inbox clutter. Such automation leverages hierarchical folder structures effectively, further strengthening the overall organization and clarity of users' mailboxes.

Additionally, hierarchical folders significantly enhance administrative management in enterprise or organizational environments. Administrators can define and enforce standardized folder structures across multiple users or groups, ensuring consistency and facilitating compliance with organizational policies or legal requirements. Folder standardization helps organizations efficiently manage compliance processes, as specific communications related to regulatory or legal requirements can be routed and retained within clearly designated folders. Centralized server-side management simplifies administrative oversight, allowing organizations to implement effective data retention and archival policies.

Security considerations further underline the importance of IMAP's hierarchical folder management capabilities. Administrators can employ access control lists (ACLs) at the folder level, defining explicit permissions for user groups or individual users to access or modify folder contents. Access controls enhance mailbox security by restricting visibility and actions on sensitive or confidential folders. Implementing such fine-grained permissions allows organizations to balance accessibility requirements with data protection, ensuring that only authorized personnel access sensitive organizational communications.

IMAP's hierarchical folder organization capability also integrates seamlessly with archival and backup processes. Administrators can configure automated backup systems that preserve entire folder structures, including nested subfolders, to facilitate efficient disaster recovery or mailbox restoration processes. Restoring entire folder hierarchies significantly accelerates recovery after incidents such as accidental deletions, data corruption, or cybersecurity breaches, ensuring minimal disruption and quick resumption of normal email activities.

Performance optimization represents another vital aspect of hierarchical folder management. Well-organized, structured mailboxes typically exhibit better performance, reduced synchronization delays, and quicker message retrieval compared to unorganized mailboxes with excessive emails in a single folder. Administrators often encourage users to manage mailbox structures proactively, periodically reviewing and optimizing folders to ensure continued performance. Additionally, email servers frequently implement indexing solutions tailored specifically to hierarchical folder management, ensuring rapid message retrieval and search efficiency even within deeply nested folder structures.

As digital communications evolve continuously, maintaining effective hierarchical folder organization remains critical to productive email management. The flexibility, synchronization capabilities, automation possibilities, security features, and administrative benefits provided by IMAP's hierarchical folders offer powerful solutions to challenges arising from escalating email volumes. Users and organizations utilizing IMAP's robust hierarchical folder features experience significant improvements in email organization, productivity, and security, ensuring efficient management of digital communications in today's complex technological landscape.

Searching and Filtering with IMAP

The capability to effectively search and filter email content is a fundamental aspect of email management within the Internet Message Access Protocol (IMAP). As email volumes continue to grow exponentially, efficient searching and accurate filtering are crucial for maintaining productivity, organization, and accessibility of information. IMAP addresses these needs by providing powerful server-side searching and filtering mechanisms, significantly enhancing users' abilities to manage, locate, and access messages swiftly, even within extensive mailboxes containing thousands or tens of thousands of emails.

IMAP's server-side searching allows email clients to quickly retrieve messages matching specific criteria directly from the email server, without requiring the client to download all messages first. This approach provides significant performance benefits compared to older protocols that demanded clients download full email content prior to initiating local searches. Server-side searching within IMAP can dramatically reduce network traffic, optimize bandwidth usage, and accelerate response times, especially in environments where bandwidth constraints exist, such as mobile or remote networks.

IMAP searching is highly sophisticated and versatile, supporting numerous search criteria that users can combine to produce precise and accurate search results. Common IMAP search parameters include sender and recipient email addresses, subject lines, specific keywords or phrases within message bodies, message dates or date ranges, message sizes, and various flags or message statuses, such as read, unread, flagged, or answered messages. By combining these criteria, users can execute intricate queries—for instance, locating all unread emails sent from a particular sender containing specific keywords during a defined period. Such powerful and flexible searching capability significantly reduces the time required for users to locate critical communications, thereby improving overall productivity and responsiveness.

Moreover, IMAP searching integrates seamlessly with the hierarchical folder structures that characterize IMAP mailbox management. Users can specify search scopes within particular folders or subfolders, restricting search results to selected mailbox locations, thus refining searches and eliminating irrelevant results. Folder-specific searches are particularly advantageous for users who maintain well-organized folder structures, as they allow rapid identification of specific communications related to particular projects, clients, or topics without unnecessarily expanding the search across the entire mailbox.

Filtering, closely related to searching, represents another essential capability provided by IMAP to enhance email management efficiency. Filtering involves automatically categorizing incoming messages according to predefined rules or criteria, organizing emails systematically into designated folders upon arrival. IMAP-compatible email clients typically support advanced filtering mechanisms, enabling users to create detailed, condition-based rules to automatically sort incoming messages. These rules can consider various attributes, including senders, recipients, subjects, keywords, attachment presence, message size, or dates, directing matching emails immediately into specified folders or applying message flags and statuses accordingly.

Automated filtering significantly streamlines email workflows, reducing manual organizational tasks and minimizing inbox clutter. Users can configure filters to automatically route less urgent or informational messages away from primary inboxes, reserving inboxes primarily for high-priority or actionable emails. This focused management approach helps users avoid becoming overwhelmed by large volumes of incoming messages, enabling greater concentration on critical tasks and enhancing overall productivity.

IMAP's filtering capabilities extend beyond simple organizational tasks, providing valuable assistance in managing unwanted or unsolicited emails, such as spam or marketing communications. Server-side filtering integration with spam detection systems allows IMAP servers to automatically direct suspected spam messages into dedicated folders, significantly reducing inbox disruptions and improving email security. Users benefit from reduced exposure to phishing attempts, malware threats, and other cyber risks associated with unwanted messages. By leveraging advanced server-side spam filtering, IMAP contributes substantially to maintaining secure, organized, and productive email environments.

Furthermore, IMAP's searching and filtering capabilities play essential roles in compliance management within organizational contexts. Enterprises frequently implement strict data retention policies or compliance procedures, requiring specific types of messages to be retained, archived, or categorized systematically. IMAP supports compliance requirements by enabling administrators to implement server-side rules or filters that automatically route, archive, or retain messages matching particular compliance criteria. Automated compliance filtering ensures consistent adherence to organizational or regulatory requirements, reducing administrative overhead and facilitating straightforward compliance audits or investigations.

Performance optimization constitutes another critical aspect of searching and filtering with IMAP, particularly in extensive or large-scale mailboxes. IMAP servers frequently incorporate advanced indexing solutions, maintaining structured indexes of message attributes, metadata, and textual content to facilitate rapid and efficient searching and filtering processes. Indexed searches significantly accelerate retrieval speeds, enabling almost instantaneous responses to even complex search queries. Administrators often proactively monitor indexing performance, periodically optimizing server indexes to ensure continued high performance and responsive mailbox management.

Modern developments in IMAP protocol extensions further enhance searching and filtering capabilities, continually adapting to user demands and evolving technological environments. Extensions such as IMAP SEARCHRES (Search Results) or ESEARCH (Extended Search) provide enhanced search functionalities, including improved efficiency, extended result management, and server-side caching of recent search results, significantly reducing resource usage and improving search responsiveness. Such extensions enable IMAP searching and filtering to remain responsive, scalable, and effective, even as email repositories continue to expand dramatically.

Overall, IMAP's advanced server-side searching and automated filtering capabilities provide users with powerful tools for effective email management. Robust search functionalities, precise filtering rules, hierarchical folder integration, compliance support, spam prevention, and optimized performance collectively enhance user productivity, reduce manual workload, streamline compliance management, and secure email environments. As digital communication volumes continue increasing, effective searching and filtering remain critical to efficient email management, highlighting IMAP's continued significance in contemporary digital communication practices.

Message Flags and Attributes

In IMAP (Internet Message Access Protocol), message flags and attributes constitute a powerful and essential feature enabling users to manage, classify, and interact efficiently with their email communications. These flags represent metadata attached to email messages, indicating specific states, statuses, or categories assigned to messages. Unlike previous email protocols, IMAP manages these flags directly on the mail server, ensuring consistent and synchronized visibility of message statuses across multiple client devices and platforms. As email volumes grow and become increasingly complex, the ability to accurately track, prioritize, and organize messages through flags and attributes significantly improves user productivity, workflow management, and overall email experience.

IMAP defines a range of standard message flags that email clients commonly use to represent message states. Among these standard flags, one of the most frequently utilized is the Seen flag, indicating whether a message has been read or remains unread. Marking messages as read or unread is fundamental for users, helping them quickly determine which messages require attention or action. Since IMAP synchronizes message states across devices, users who read an email on one device will automatically see the same message marked as read on all other connected clients, ensuring uniform visibility and preventing confusion or redundant processing of the same message.

Another critical standard flag provided by IMAP is the Answered flag, denoting that the user has replied to a particular message. Tracking answered emails helps users quickly identify which communications have already been addressed, facilitating efficient workflow management and reducing redundancy. Similarly, the Flagged attribute, often represented visually as a star or similar symbol, is utilized by users to mark emails requiring special attention, follow-up, or action at a later time. The Flagged status provides users with immediate visual indicators of priority or importance, enabling them to manage their tasks and email workflows proactively and efficiently.

The Deleted flag is another vital attribute in IMAP, marking messages that users intend to remove from their mailbox. Unlike protocols that immediately remove deleted emails from servers, IMAP treats deletion as a multi-stage process. Messages marked as deleted remain visible until the mailbox undergoes an explicit purge or expunge operation, permanently removing deleted messages. This staged deletion process provides users with valuable safeguards, allowing them opportunities to review or recover messages mistakenly marked as deleted before permanent removal occurs. Administrators and users alike benefit from this approach, minimizing the risk of unintended data loss.

Additionally, IMAP includes the Draft flag, indicating emails that users have composed but not yet finalized or sent. Draft messages frequently reside within a specialized Drafts folder, synchronized across client devices, enabling users to seamlessly resume composing messages from any connected device. By managing drafts centrally on the server, IMAP ensures flexibility, mobility, and continuity, essential for users frequently switching between different devices or locations.

Beyond standard flags, IMAP also allows user-defined or custom flags. Custom flags provide users and organizations with additional flexibility to classify messages according to specific needs, organizational policies, or workflows. Users can define unique flags, such as Project-X, Invoice, or Urgent-Client, allowing precise categorization and rapid identification of relevant messages. Custom flags significantly enhance mailbox organization, enabling users to quickly retrieve and manage groups of related emails according to personalized or organizational priorities.

The synchronization of message flags and attributes across multiple devices represents one of IMAP's key strengths. When users alter the flag status of messages—for instance, marking a message as read, flagged, answered, or deleted—the updated status synchronizes immediately with the IMAP server. The server subsequently propagates these changes across all connected client devices. Immediate synchronization ensures consistency and prevents confusion resulting from discrepancies in message states across devices, enhancing user experience, productivity, and efficiency, especially for users frequently managing email from multiple locations or using mobile devices.

Moreover, IMAP's server-side management of flags and attributes facilitates powerful searching and filtering functionalities. Users can execute server-side searches based explicitly on flag criteria, retrieving specific subsets of messages efficiently, such as unread emails, flagged messages, or unanswered communications. Server-side searching based on flags significantly improves user efficiency by rapidly narrowing results, even in mailboxes containing large volumes of email.

In organizational or enterprise contexts, IMAP flags also contribute significantly to compliance management, task assignment, and collaboration workflows. Enterprises can leverage message flags to enforce standardized procedures, tracking message status throughout various workflow stages, such as approval processes, compliance reviews, or customer support inquiries. By systematically applying flags to messages as they progress through organizational workflows, administrators and managers maintain clear oversight and visibility into critical communications, streamlining processes, and improving operational efficiency.

Administrators can further leverage message flags in retention management, archiving, and backup strategies. For example, messages flagged as important, compliance-related, or confidential might receive special retention policies or be automatically included in regular backup schedules. Message flags thus become an integral part of comprehensive data management and protection strategies, ensuring critical communications receive appropriate handling and safeguarding.

From a technical perspective, IMAP servers manage flags efficiently by maintaining dedicated metadata repositories, frequently indexed for rapid access and synchronization performance. These indexes enhance performance when users perform flag-related queries, searches, or updates, providing instantaneous responses even within extensive email collections. Performance optimization through indexing ensures responsiveness, scalability, and reliability, critical characteristics for modern email management.

IMAP extensions further expand the functionality of message flags and attributes, continually adapting the protocol to evolving user needs and technological developments. Advanced IMAP extensions enhance flag synchronization efficiency, reduce network bandwidth usage, and offer additional custom flag management features. By continuously adapting and expanding capabilities, IMAP remains responsive to the increasingly sophisticated requirements of modern digital communication practices.

Message flags and attributes within IMAP represent a robust, essential capability, significantly enhancing email management efficiency, productivity, and organization. The consistent synchronization, flexibility of custom flags, advanced search integration, and critical role in workflow management collectively ensure IMAP remains indispensable for contemporary email users navigating increasingly complex digital communication environments.

Synchronization Mechanisms in IMAP

Synchronization is a foundational aspect of IMAP (Internet Message Access Protocol), enabling users to consistently access and manage their emails across multiple devices and platforms. Unlike previous email protocols, IMAP emphasizes real-time synchronization of message states, attributes, and mailbox structures, ensuring that users experience seamless and uniform email management, regardless of which device or client they use. This synchronization capability fundamentally shapes how individuals and organizations interact with their email systems, improving efficiency, productivity, and reliability.

IMAP achieves synchronization primarily through continuous, persistent client-server connections, allowing real-time updates of mailbox states and message attributes. When a user performs actions such as reading, replying, deleting, or moving emails between folders, these actions are communicated instantly to the IMAP server. The server immediately updates its internal mailbox state accordingly, then propagates these changes to all other connected client devices. This instant synchronization ensures that users have the same view of their mailbox from any device or location, eliminating inconsistencies or redundant management tasks that were common with earlier protocols such as POP3.

At the technical level, IMAP employs various mechanisms to facilitate efficient and responsive synchronization. One critical feature is IMAP's unique message identifiers (UIDs). Each message stored on the IMAP server is assigned a permanent and unique identifier, distinct from the sequential message numbers used by earlier email protocols. UIDs remain constant throughout a message's lifecycle, even when messages are moved between folders or when other messages are deleted, added, or rearranged. This persistent identification enables precise synchronization between the client and server, allowing IMAP clients to accurately track and synchronize changes even in complex scenarios involving mailbox modifications.

Another essential IMAP synchronization mechanism is the implementation of mailbox state tokens or sequence numbers. IMAP servers typically maintain sequence numbers representing the current state of each mailbox, updating these tokens whenever changes occur, such as message additions, deletions, or modifications of flags and attributes. IMAP clients leverage these state tokens during synchronization sessions to quickly determine whether mailbox content or attributes have changed since their last synchronization. If mailbox state tokens indicate no changes, synchronization becomes efficient, with minimal data transfer, significantly reducing bandwidth consumption and enhancing responsiveness, particularly valuable in mobile or bandwidth-constrained environments.

A key IMAP synchronization extension known as IMAP IDLE further enhances real-time responsiveness. The IMAP IDLE command allows email clients to maintain open connections with the IMAP server, awaiting server-side notifications of mailbox changes, such as new message arrivals or flag updates. Instead of continuously polling the server, clients remain in an idle state, passively awaiting server-generated notifications. Upon detecting mailbox updates, the server instantly pushes notifications to clients, prompting them to synchronize the updated information immediately. IMAP IDLE drastically improves efficiency, reduces network bandwidth usage, and delivers instant message updates to users, a vital capability for real-time responsiveness, especially on mobile devices or resource-constrained networks.

Synchronization mechanisms in IMAP also encompass efficient partial synchronization capabilities. In scenarios involving large mailboxes or limited network bandwidth, complete mailbox synchronization can become resource-intensive and inefficient. IMAP provides selective synchronization features, allowing clients to download and synchronize only specific subsets of mailbox data, such as message headers, recent emails, or messages matching certain criteria or flags. Partial synchronization significantly improves performance, reduces bandwidth demands, and enhances user experience, enabling users to rapidly access relevant messages without delays associated with full mailbox synchronization.

Synchronization within IMAP extends beyond message states and mailbox structures, encompassing folder hierarchies and attributes as well. Users frequently manage complex folder structures to organize emails systematically by projects, topics, or priorities. IMAP ensures that folder creations, renaming, deletions, or reorganizations synchronize immediately across client devices, maintaining consistent and intuitive mailbox organization. This synchronization consistency ensures that users retain familiar mailbox structures regardless of the device or client used, significantly improving user experience, productivity, and organizational efficiency.

Effective synchronization also relies heavily on robust server-side data management. IMAP servers typically implement sophisticated indexing and metadata management strategies, ensuring rapid synchronization responses even in large-scale or enterprise environments. Indexing structures such as databases or specialized data stores track message attributes, unique identifiers, folder states, and mailbox changes, enabling servers to quickly respond to synchronization requests from clients. High-performance indexing optimizes synchronization efficiency, ensuring minimal latency, rapid response times, and consistent synchronization performance across diverse client environments.

From a security perspective, synchronization mechanisms in IMAP require secure communication channels, particularly since synchronization involves frequent, sensitive exchanges between clients and servers. IMAP servers typically utilize encryption protocols such as SSL/TLS to secure synchronization interactions, ensuring that message states, attributes, and mailbox metadata remain confidential during synchronization processes. Secure synchronization prevents potential interception, unauthorized access, or manipulation of synchronized data, providing essential safeguards for user privacy and email data security.

Additionally, synchronization mechanisms play a critical role in disaster recovery and mailbox backup strategies. Since IMAP maintains message data and mailbox states centrally on the server, synchronization inherently simplifies backup and recovery processes. Administrators can leverage synchronization mechanisms to efficiently restore mailbox data and attributes after incidents such as data corruption, accidental deletions, or server failures. Rapid synchronization after recovery operations ensures minimal disruption and rapid restoration of mailbox integrity, reinforcing resilience and reliability within IMAP environments.

IMAP synchronization continues to evolve through protocol extensions, responding actively to changing technological demands and user expectations. Advanced synchronization extensions provide enhanced capabilities such as efficient synchronization of large attachments, improved incremental synchronization algorithms, and more granular control over synchronization processes. Continuous innovation ensures IMAP synchronization mechanisms remain responsive, scalable, and effective in supporting contemporary digital communication needs.

Synchronization mechanisms in IMAP represent a fundamental strength, significantly enhancing email management consistency, responsiveness, and productivity. Persistent client-server connections, unique identifiers, mailbox state tokens, IMAP IDLE, partial synchronization capabilities, secure communication, robust indexing, and disaster recovery integration collectively deliver synchronization excellence, ensuring that IMAP remains indispensable for modern digital communication environments.

Managing Attachments and MIME Types

Managing attachments and MIME (Multipurpose Internet Mail Extensions) types represents a fundamental component within IMAP (Internet Message Access Protocol), greatly influencing the flexibility, usability, and efficiency of email communication. With the constant exchange of multimedia, documents, and various file types, modern email systems must proficiently handle diverse content seamlessly. IMAP, coupled with MIME, provides sophisticated mechanisms that allow email clients and servers to effectively store, retrieve, interpret, and manage attachments, ensuring consistency and accessibility across different platforms and devices.

Attachments have become ubiquitous in email communications, enabling users to share documents, images, videos, presentations, and other file formats directly through their email systems. However, managing attachments effectively introduces technical and usability considerations, especially as attachments vary significantly in size, content type, and complexity. IMAP supports robust handling of attachments by storing message content, including attachments, centrally on servers, allowing users to download, preview, or manipulate attachments consistently from any client device. By centrally managing attachments, IMAP significantly reduces redundancies and ensures uniform access, crucial for users frequently accessing their emails across multiple devices such as desktops, tablets, and mobile phones.

MIME plays a critical complementary role in attachment management within IMAP environments. As email was originally designed primarily for plain-text communications, MIME was introduced to extend email capabilities to handle diverse content types beyond basic text. MIME specifies standardized methods to encode, decode, and interpret various types of content, including binary data such as images, audio files, videos, applications, and complex multipart documents. Through MIME encoding, attachments are transformed into standardized textual representations, making them suitable for transmission via email protocols such as IMAP. When recipients open these emails, MIME decoding processes ensure attachments are accurately reconstructed into their original binary formats, seamlessly displayed or opened in corresponding applications.

IMAP servers utilize MIME headers extensively to facilitate attachment management and content identification. Each attachment within an email contains specific MIME headers describing its content type, encoding mechanism, filename, and disposition information. Content type headers define precise classifications of attachments, such as image/jpeg, application/pdf, audio/mp3, or text/html, enabling email clients to determine appropriate handling and rendering methods. Filename and disposition headers further assist clients in recognizing attachments, guiding decisions such as automatically displaying embedded images or prompting users to download external attachments.

Efficient attachment retrieval is a key capability offered by IMAP, particularly beneficial when managing large attachments or bandwidth-constrained environments. IMAP allows selective or partial downloading of attachments, empowering users to preview or retrieve specific attachments without downloading entire messages initially. Clients can request specific MIME sections or attachment parts directly from IMAP servers, significantly enhancing responsiveness and reducing bandwidth usage. Partial retrieval proves particularly advantageous for users accessing emails on mobile devices or slow networks, allowing rapid preview and selective downloading of essential attachments without incurring unnecessary data transfers.

Attachment management efficiency also involves considerations regarding storage optimization and mailbox size management. As attachments frequently consume substantial storage resources, especially when large multimedia files or extensive documents are exchanged, IMAP mailbox quotas and storage capacities become significant administrative concerns. Effective management involves strategies such as automatic attachment archiving, compressing attachments, or implementing size-based attachment policies. Administrators frequently implement automated tools integrated with IMAP servers that periodically archive older or infrequently accessed attachments, freeing mailbox storage and optimizing performance without sacrificing accessibility.

Security considerations are integral when managing attachments, given attachments' frequent association with cybersecurity threats such as malware, ransomware, or phishing attacks. IMAP environments incorporate security measures to detect, filter, or quarantine suspicious attachments proactively. Attachment filtering rules analyze MIME types, file extensions, or embedded content, automatically preventing potentially dangerous attachments from reaching user inboxes. Server-side antivirus and malware scanning complement MIME-based attachment filtering, ensuring attachments remain safe and secure for user interactions. Additionally, IMAP supports encryption protocols such as SSL/TLS to ensure attachment transmission remains secure, protecting sensitive attachment content from interception or unauthorized access during transit between clients and servers.

User productivity and workflow efficiency benefit significantly from effective attachment management within IMAP environments. Advanced IMAP-compatible email clients frequently integrate powerful attachment handling functionalities, enabling users to drag-and-drop attachments directly into emails, preview attachments seamlessly within client interfaces, and effortlessly save attachments to cloud storage or local directories. IMAP's centralized attachment management facilitates synchronization of these user interactions across multiple devices, ensuring consistent attachment accessibility and reducing redundant actions.

Organizational and enterprise environments frequently leverage IMAP's attachment management capabilities to enhance compliance management and record retention strategies. Attachments regularly constitute critical evidence or documentation required for regulatory compliance, legal audits, or organizational record-keeping policies.

IMAP servers support comprehensive attachment archiving strategies, ensuring attachments are systematically retained, indexed, and accessible for compliance or legal discovery purposes. Integrating IMAP attachment management with dedicated archival solutions facilitates efficient retrieval and management of attachments according to defined retention policies or regulatory requirements.

Performance optimization represents another essential dimension of managing attachments and MIME types effectively within IMAP environments. IMAP servers often implement sophisticated indexing solutions, tracking attachment metadata, MIME headers, and content attributes. These indexes enhance attachment retrieval speeds, ensuring rapid, efficient responses to user requests even within extensive mailbox repositories containing thousands of attachment-rich messages. Regular performance monitoring and indexing optimization maintain high responsiveness and scalability, enabling IMAP environments to efficiently support large-scale attachment handling demands characteristic of modern digital communication practices.

Continuous advancements in MIME standards and IMAP protocol extensions further enhance attachment management capabilities, responding actively to evolving technological requirements and user expectations. Innovations such as improved MIME type recognition, enhanced attachment compression methods, and optimized partial retrieval algorithms ensure IMAP remains highly capable, responsive, and adaptive in managing diverse attachment content efficiently.

Attachment management and MIME type handling within IMAP environments significantly influence modern email communication effectiveness. Centralized storage, selective retrieval, MIME integration, security considerations, compliance support, productivity enhancements, performance optimization, and continuous innovation collectively ensure IMAP maintains its vital role in efficiently managing the increasingly diverse and complex attachment content characteristic of contemporary digital communication.

IMAP Extensions and Their Uses

IMAP, or Internet Message Access Protocol, provides powerful functionality in email management, but it continually evolves through protocol extensions designed to meet emerging user needs, address technical challenges, and adapt to changing digital environments. IMAP extensions are standardized enhancements that augment the core IMAP capabilities, introducing new functionalities, optimizing existing processes, and ensuring IMAP remains versatile, robust, and responsive to contemporary communication demands. The development and integration of these extensions significantly expand IMAP's usability, making it a continually evolving protocol highly adaptable to diverse contexts and technological innovations.

Among the notable IMAP extensions is IMAP IDLE, which enhances real-time message synchronization by enabling push-based notifications between IMAP clients and servers. Traditionally, email clients had to continuously poll servers to check for new emails, consuming considerable bandwidth and introducing latency. With IMAP IDLE, clients maintain a persistent open connection, allowing the server to immediately notify the client when new messages arrive or when changes occur in mailbox status. This push notification approach significantly reduces network traffic, improves battery efficiency on mobile devices, and provides users with instant email notifications, greatly enhancing productivity and responsiveness.

Another widely implemented IMAP extension is IMAP UIDPLUS, designed to improve message identification and synchronization efficiency. The UIDPLUS extension introduces additional commands that facilitate better client-server synchronization, especially when emails are copied or moved between mailboxes. With UIDPLUS, servers provide immediate feedback on operations like message copying or deletion, allowing clients to accurately track message identifiers without unnecessary re-synchronization processes. This significantly enhances synchronization speed and consistency, especially in large mailboxes, resulting in a smoother and more reliable email experience.

The IMAP CONDSTORE extension (Conditional Store) also plays an essential role in optimizing synchronization efficiency. CONDSTORE introduces message state tokens, enabling clients to perform conditional synchronization, retrieving only messages or metadata that changed since the previous synchronization. By eliminating redundant data transfers, this extension dramatically reduces bandwidth consumption and accelerates synchronization, particularly beneficial for mobile users or bandwidth-limited environments. CONDSTORE's conditional approach ensures IMAP clients remain efficiently synchronized without repeatedly downloading unchanged mailbox content.

IMAP QRESYNC, or Quick Resynchronization, builds upon CONDSTORE, providing even more advanced synchronization optimization. QRESYNC allows email clients to quickly and accurately synchronize mailbox states after periods of offline activity, network disruptions, or client restarts. Clients can rapidly detect which messages were deleted, added, or altered during offline periods, restoring synchronization with minimal data exchange. This rapid re-synchronization capability substantially improves user experience, significantly reducing delays in mailbox updates and improving overall responsiveness, especially in mobile or intermittent connectivity scenarios.

Another valuable extension, IMAP SORT, enhances mailbox management by enabling server-side sorting of email messages based on various criteria. IMAP SORT allows clients to request sorted message lists directly from servers, eliminating the need for clients to download complete message data before sorting locally. Sorting criteria supported include dates, senders, recipients, subjects, and message sizes, among others. Server-side sorting significantly accelerates mailbox operations, improves performance, and reduces client-side resource consumption, providing users with immediate, organized access to their messages, especially beneficial in extensive mailbox environments.

Similarly, the IMAP THREAD extension provides advanced capabilities for managing email conversations. THREAD enables servers to group related messages into conversation threads based on standardized algorithms, presenting coherent views of email discussions to users. Clients leveraging THREAD extensions can efficiently display threaded conversations, allowing users to follow complex discussions more intuitively. This enhanced conversational context reduces clutter, simplifies navigation, and significantly improves productivity when managing extensive email interactions across multiple participants.

The IMAP SEARCHRES (Search Results) and ESEARCH (Extended Search) extensions significantly enhance IMAP's searching capabilities, allowing more efficient and sophisticated server-side search operations. SEARCHRES enables servers to retain results of previous search queries, permitting clients to perform additional filtering or subsequent operations on the retained results, eliminating repeated server-side searches. ESEARCH provides extended search functionalities, allowing servers to return detailed metadata about search results, such as message counts or unique identifiers, significantly reducing data exchange and improving search efficiency. These extensions empower users with rapid, precise, and flexible searching, especially beneficial when handling large email volumes or performing complex searches.

IMAP METADATA, another valuable extension, provides structured management of mailbox metadata beyond standard message attributes. This extension allows users or administrators to store, retrieve, and manage custom mailbox annotations or configuration data on IMAP servers. Mailbox metadata could include custom tags, client-specific mailbox settings, or additional information supporting organizational policies. By supporting structured metadata management, IMAP METADATA significantly enhances mailbox customization, administrative management, and client-specific mailbox behaviors, improving overall flexibility and user experience.

Additionally, the IMAP SPECIAL-USE extension assists users and clients in identifying special mailboxes, such as Sent, Drafts, Trash, or Archive folders. SPECIAL-USE provides standardized mechanisms allowing servers to designate mailbox roles explicitly, simplifying client-side mailbox configuration and enhancing user experience by automatically mapping these special-purpose mailboxes consistently across multiple devices or client applications. Clearly identifying special mailboxes eliminates confusion, streamlines client configurations, and significantly improves email management usability and consistency.

The IMAP COMPRESS extension further contributes to efficiency, enabling compression of data exchanged between IMAP clients and servers. COMPRESS reduces bandwidth usage, significantly accelerating synchronization, especially beneficial when accessing email from mobile devices or networks with limited bandwidth capacity. Implementing data compression improves synchronization speed, reduces latency, conserves network resources, and enhances overall email responsiveness, providing users with smoother, faster, and more reliable email interactions.

IMAP extensions remain continuously evolving standards, actively developed by technical communities to address emerging challenges and meet future digital communication needs. Emerging extensions regularly address security improvements, performance optimization, additional mailbox management capabilities, or enhanced user experiences. As digital communication environments grow increasingly complex, diverse, and demanding, IMAP's extensibility ensures it remains highly adaptable, resilient, and responsive, capable of efficiently supporting the diverse communication requirements of individuals, enterprises, and global organizations alike.

Understanding IMAP IDLE

IMAP IDLE is a fundamental extension within the Internet Message Access Protocol (IMAP) designed specifically to facilitate real-time synchronization between email clients and servers. As email has become a critical form of instantaneous communication, the demand for rapid, responsive email delivery has significantly increased. IMAP IDLE addresses this need effectively by enabling instant notifications to email clients whenever new messages arrive, eliminating the necessity for periodic polling. This feature provides immediate visibility of incoming messages, considerably enhancing the user experience and efficiency of modern email systems.

Traditionally, email clients relied on periodic polling mechanisms to check servers for new messages. This involved repeatedly initiating connections to query the email server at set intervals, typically ranging from a few minutes to several hours. Polling often led to significant delays between the actual arrival of an email and the time users became aware of its presence. Additionally, continuous polling resulted in unnecessary consumption of network bandwidth and increased battery drain on mobile devices, particularly problematic for users operating on limited or expensive network connections.

IMAP IDLE fundamentally revolutionized this conventional polling model. Rather than periodically querying the server, the IMAP client establishes a persistent connection that remains open indefinitely. When an IMAP client initiates the IDLE command, it effectively informs the server that it is ready and waiting for immediate notifications about mailbox updates. Consequently, the server maintains this active connection without the overhead of continuous reconnection attempts or repeated queries. When new messages arrive or mailbox updates occur—such as message deletions, flag changes, or message moves—the IMAP server immediately sends notifications directly to the connected client, enabling instant synchronization.

The IMAP IDLE mechanism significantly optimizes bandwidth usage compared to polling methods. By maintaining a persistent open connection, IMAP IDLE greatly reduces the repeated overhead associated with setting up and tearing down connections. Instead of continuously initiating new requests and processing server responses, clients remain passively connected, awaiting server-initiated notifications. As a result, network traffic and bandwidth consumption are dramatically minimized, making IMAP IDLE particularly beneficial for mobile users relying on cellular networks or users in environments with limited connectivity.

Moreover, the immediate notification provided by IMAP IDLE profoundly enhances email responsiveness and user productivity. Users can instantly view incoming messages, reply rapidly to urgent communications, and maintain real-time email interactions similar to instant messaging systems. This immediate responsiveness is crucial in business environments, where delays in email communications can affect critical decision-making processes, customer interactions, or urgent issue resolution. IMAP IDLE ensures that email clients remain continuously updated without delays, meeting the demanding expectations of today's always-connected digital environment.

The effectiveness of IMAP IDLE extends significantly to mobile email usage scenarios. Mobile devices often face inherent limitations related to battery life, network constraints, and connectivity fluctuations. IMAP IDLE directly addresses these challenges by significantly reducing battery consumption through eliminating repeated connection attempts inherent in polling. Mobile clients utilizing IMAP IDLE can remain efficiently synchronized with the server, receiving instantaneous notifications without excessive energy usage. This efficiency allows mobile users to enjoy real-time email updates without adversely affecting battery life, a crucial consideration in the design of mobile email applications.

Implementing IMAP IDLE successfully also involves certain considerations related to server scalability and resource management. Maintaining numerous simultaneous persistent connections from multiple clients can increase resource usage on IMAP servers. Servers must manage open connections efficiently, requiring well-optimized architecture, robust network infrastructure, and careful resource allocation to support large-scale deployments. Advanced IMAP server implementations typically incorporate optimized resource management techniques, such as connection multiplexing, load balancing, and scalable server architectures, ensuring reliable performance even with extensive concurrent usage of the IMAP IDLE mechanism.

Client-side implementation of IMAP IDLE requires appropriate integration within email software applications. Clients must actively manage persistent connections, periodically issuing IDLE commands and managing reconnections effectively in the event of network interruptions, connectivity losses, or server restarts. Effective client implementations ensure seamless continuity of IMAP IDLE functionality, automatically re-establishing connections and re-synchronizing mailbox states quickly after disruptions, maintaining uninterrupted real-time email synchronization and enhancing user experience.

Security remains a critical aspect when deploying IMAP IDLE due to persistent open connections between email clients and servers. IMAP IDLE communications typically occur over secure, encrypted channels utilizing SSL/TLS protocols, ensuring that real-time notifications and mailbox updates remain confidential during transmission. Encryption safeguards against potential interception or unauthorized access attempts, essential for maintaining privacy and integrity of email communications. Administrators must carefully configure IMAP servers to enforce secure communication standards consistently, guaranteeing IMAP IDLE communications remain protected against evolving cybersecurity threats.

In enterprise environments, IMAP IDLE also contributes positively to compliance, auditability, and administrative oversight. Real-time notifications provide immediate visibility into mailbox activities, enabling administrators to effectively monitor and log mailbox events. Continuous, instant mailbox updates facilitate swift identification and responses to potential security incidents, unauthorized access attempts, or policy violations. Additionally, IMAP IDLE's real-time responsiveness supports compliance processes requiring timely tracking, archiving, or retrieval of specific emails for regulatory or legal purposes, enhancing overall administrative management.

IMAP IDLE continues evolving through ongoing IMAP protocol advancements and extensions designed to optimize performance further, enhance scalability, and address emerging user demands or technological developments. Innovations such as optimized reconnection mechanisms, intelligent handling of network interruptions, and efficient resource management strategies ensure IMAP IDLE remains highly effective, scalable, and adaptable in meeting future digital communication challenges.

Overall, IMAP IDLE profoundly enhances the email management experience, delivering real-time responsiveness, significant bandwidth and battery efficiencies, mobile optimization, scalability support, secure communication, and administrative advantages. Its role in contemporary email systems underscores IMAP's continued relevance and adaptability, positioning IMAP IDLE as an indispensable feature enabling modern, efficient, and productive email communications.

Enhancing Performance with IMAP Compression

Performance optimization remains a critical aspect of modern email communication systems, and IMAP compression is a key enhancement specifically designed to improve efficiency, responsiveness, and resource utilization within the Internet Message Access Protocol (IMAP). As email usage continues to grow, particularly with increasing multimedia attachments, embedded graphics, and lengthy textual content, bandwidth consumption becomes a significant consideration. IMAP compression addresses these challenges by effectively reducing the size of data transferred between email clients and servers, significantly accelerating synchronization, improving responsiveness, and conserving network resources.

IMAP compression operates by applying standardized data compression algorithms to the information exchanged between IMAP clients and servers. When IMAP compression is activated, all commands, responses, message headers, metadata, and message bodies transmitted during a session are compressed before transmission, and subsequently decompressed upon reception. The primary goal of compression is to minimize the volume of data that must traverse the network, thus decreasing latency and enhancing synchronization speeds. This reduction in data transfer is especially beneficial when email clients operate on mobile networks, remote locations, or constrained bandwidth environments.

One of the primary algorithms employed by IMAP compression implementations is DEFLATE, a highly efficient and widely supported compression method. DEFLATE combines two powerful techniques— LZ77 compression and Huffman coding—to identify repetitive patterns within data streams and replace them with shorter, symbolic representations. Through DEFLATE compression, IMAP achieves substantial data size reductions, frequently shrinking transmitted data by more than fifty percent. The effectiveness of DEFLATE contributes significantly to bandwidth conservation, reducing data costs for users, particularly those on cellular or metered connections, and accelerating synchronization processes across diverse client environments.

The immediate benefit of IMAP compression is evident in improved email synchronization performance. When compression is enabled, users experience rapid mailbox updates, shorter loading times, and faster message retrieval. Email clients leveraging compression display quicker response times, even when retrieving large volumes of email messages, extensive attachments, or rich media content. Faster synchronization enhances productivity and responsiveness, crucial in business environments where efficient access to email communication directly impacts decision-making, customer service, and operational workflows. Compression ensures that email interactions remain smooth, fluid, and consistently responsive across varying network conditions.

Additionally, IMAP compression significantly enhances mobile email performance. Mobile devices frequently operate in bandwidth-limited or unstable network environments, relying on cellular connections or public Wi-Fi networks. Under such conditions, synchronization latency and excessive data usage can negatively affect user experience. IMAP compression alleviates these issues by reducing data transfer sizes, thus accelerating synchronization processes and minimizing data consumption. Users benefit from quicker email updates, lower data charges, and extended battery life due to reduced radio usage, all of which greatly enhance mobile usability and productivity.

Beyond performance improvements, IMAP compression also contributes to improved server efficiency and scalability. Compressing data transmitted to multiple concurrent clients significantly reduces server bandwidth consumption and resource usage. IMAP servers handling thousands of simultaneous client connections can achieve substantial bandwidth savings by implementing compression, allowing server infrastructure to scale more effectively. Reduced data transmission volumes lower network overhead, enabling servers to handle larger client populations without necessitating proportional increases in bandwidth or network resources, resulting in cost savings and optimized infrastructure utilization.

Effective deployment of IMAP compression involves specific technical considerations to ensure robust performance. Servers must be configured properly to support compression capabilities, enabling negotiated compression sessions when requested by clients. Similarly, clients must explicitly request compression support during the initial connection negotiation with the server. Once compression parameters are negotiated successfully, all subsequent client-server interactions during the session are automatically compressed. Proper implementation ensures seamless compatibility, enabling IMAP clients and servers from diverse vendors to communicate effectively using standardized compression methods.

Security considerations also accompany IMAP compression deployment. Compressed IMAP sessions typically operate within secure channels protected by encryption protocols such as SSL/TLS. Encryption ensures that compressed data remains secure during transmission, protecting sensitive email content and metadata from potential interception or unauthorized access attempts. Administrators must carefully configure secure IMAP connections, ensuring compression does not inadvertently introduce vulnerabilities or weaken encryption security. Well-implemented IMAP compression, integrated with robust encryption mechanisms, ensures that performance optimizations do not compromise security standards essential for protecting user data confidentiality and integrity.

IMAP compression is particularly advantageous within enterprise email management environments. Large-scale organizational deployments regularly involve extensive email repositories, significant attachment volumes, and high client concurrency. Implementing IMAP compression within enterprise infrastructures dramatically enhances synchronization performance, reducing bandwidth expenses, optimizing infrastructure resources, and improving user productivity across large user populations. Administrators benefit from enhanced scalability, reduced infrastructure costs, and optimized network utilization, essential factors for managing extensive email infrastructures cost-effectively and efficiently.

The development and standardization of IMAP compression continue evolving through ongoing IMAP protocol enhancements and extensions. Emerging innovations include improved compression algorithms offering higher efficiency, adaptive compression mechanisms dynamically adjusting compression levels according to network conditions or content types, and optimized handling of multimedia attachments or structured message content. These ongoing developments ensure IMAP compression remains responsive, scalable, and adaptable, addressing evolving technological requirements, user expectations, and communication complexities characteristic of modern email environments.

Advanced IMAP clients increasingly incorporate intelligent mechanisms to leverage compression effectively. For example, clients dynamically enable compression based on current network conditions, activating compression automatically when accessing email from mobile networks or low-bandwidth environments, and selectively disabling compression when operating within high-bandwidth, low-latency connections where compression overhead may outweigh benefits. Intelligent, context-aware compression implementations significantly enhance usability, ensuring optimal performance tailored dynamically to user contexts, network characteristics, and email usage scenarios.

Enhanced logging, monitoring, and reporting mechanisms frequently accompany IMAP compression deployments, providing administrators detailed visibility into compression efficiency, bandwidth savings, and resource utilization improvements. Comprehensive monitoring facilitates ongoing optimization, enabling administrators to fine-tune compression settings dynamically, address performance bottlenecks, and ensure continuous improvement of synchronization responsiveness and infrastructure efficiency.

IMAP compression significantly transforms the email management experience, providing substantial performance optimizations, bandwidth savings, mobile enhancements, scalability advantages, security integrations, and intelligent usage contexts. Its essential role underscores IMAP's continued adaptability and responsiveness, enabling efficient, productive, and optimized email communication experiences tailored precisely to contemporary digital communication demands.

Email Threading and Conversation Management

Email threading and conversation management represent crucial components in efficient email communication and organization within IMAP environments. As email usage has proliferated, users frequently engage in extensive, ongoing conversations involving multiple participants and messages. Without effective threading mechanisms, these conversations quickly become fragmented, difficult to follow, and challenging to manage efficiently. IMAP addresses this complexity by providing advanced threading capabilities that group related email messages into cohesive, structured conversations. By organizing messages logically into threaded discussions, IMAP significantly enhances readability, reduces inbox clutter, and greatly improves users' productivity and ability to manage email interactions effectively.

Threading fundamentally changes the way email messages are displayed and managed by organizing related messages into coherent groups or conversations. Messages within threads are typically arranged chronologically, allowing users to easily follow the progression of discussions from the initial message to the latest response. Email threading ensures users clearly understand the context, previous interactions, and the evolution of conversations, significantly improving comprehension, reducing confusion, and enabling quicker, more informed responses.

At a technical level, IMAP threading utilizes specific headers embedded within email messages, such as Message-ID, In-Reply-To, and References, to accurately reconstruct conversations. Each message sent includes a unique identifier (Message-ID), while replies or subsequent messages reference the original message using In-Reply-To or References headers. IMAP servers analyze these headers to detect relationships among messages, grouping them logically into conversation threads. This structured identification ensures accurate threading, even when conversations involve multiple participants or branching discussions, reliably maintaining the integrity and clarity of email interactions.

IMAP defines standardized threading algorithms such as ORDEREDSUBJECT, REFERENCES, and other advanced threading methodologies, allowing servers and clients to organize conversations effectively according to recognized standards. The REFERENCES algorithm, widely implemented within IMAP servers, uses message headers explicitly to construct threaded conversations, maintaining structural coherence even within complex, branching email discussions. Alternatively, ORDEREDSUBJECT threading groups messages sharing identical or similar subject lines into threads, particularly effective for simpler conversational structures or mailing list communications. By supporting multiple threading algorithms, IMAP provides flexible conversation management options suitable for diverse email usage scenarios and user preferences.

Efficient threading greatly simplifies inbox management by significantly reducing email clutter and redundancy. Without threading, individual replies and follow-ups typically accumulate separately within inboxes, creating fragmentation and increasing the time required for users to organize and navigate email content. Threaded views consolidate all related messages into single conversations, streamlining inbox appearance and facilitating faster message retrieval. Users quickly access entire conversation histories, easily reference previous interactions, and effortlessly maintain organized, comprehensible email environments.

Threaded conversations are particularly beneficial in professional and collaborative environments, where email interactions frequently involve extended discussions, complex decision-making processes, or project management activities. Threading enables teams to maintain clear visibility into ongoing discussions, track decisions and responses effectively, and collaborate efficiently without losing essential context. Threaded discussions reduce redundant follow-ups, prevent misunderstandings, and improve accountability by providing comprehensive conversational contexts accessible to all participants, significantly enhancing organizational communication efficiency.

IMAP threading supports robust searching and filtering functionalities, further enhancing productivity and email management effectiveness. Users easily search threaded conversations based on various criteria such as participants, subjects, keywords, or message attributes, quickly locating specific email interactions within extensive email repositories. Filtering threaded conversations by criteria such as unread messages, flagged emails, or specific participants streamlines email interactions, enabling users to focus efficiently on priority communications or unresolved discussions.

Mobile users particularly benefit from effective threading and conversation management within IMAP environments. Mobile devices frequently present limited screen space, making fragmented or cluttered inboxes challenging to navigate efficiently. Threaded views consolidate related messages, optimizing limited display areas and providing intuitive, organized conversation views, significantly enhancing mobile email usability. Users effortlessly follow complex discussions, respond promptly, and maintain productive email communications even when accessing email via constrained mobile devices or limited connectivity environments.

Advanced IMAP clients frequently implement intelligent conversation management features beyond basic threading capabilities. These advanced functionalities include automatically grouping related messages, collapsing or expanding conversation views dynamically, and providing visual indicators of unread messages within threads. Clients may also support sophisticated conversation actions, enabling users to perform bulk operations on entire threads—such as marking conversations as read, archiving discussions, or deleting completed threads—further enhancing productivity and inbox management efficiency.

Email threading additionally supports effective compliance, retention management, and auditability within organizational or enterprise contexts. Enterprises frequently require maintaining comprehensive records of email interactions for regulatory compliance, legal discovery, or internal audits. Threaded conversations provide organized, easily navigable email records, facilitating efficient retrieval, review, and archiving processes. Administrators utilize threading capabilities to implement systematic archival strategies, ensuring critical conversations are preserved accurately, comprehensively, and reliably according to established retention policies or regulatory mandates.

Performance optimization constitutes another important consideration in implementing effective threading and conversation management within IMAP environments. Servers managing extensive mailboxes frequently implement optimized threading indexing strategies, enabling rapid construction of threaded conversations even within mailboxes containing thousands of messages. Indexing structures efficiently track message relationships, headers, and conversational metadata, significantly accelerating threading processes, reducing latency, and ensuring responsive conversation views even within large-scale email deployments.

Continuous innovation and ongoing development in IMAP protocol extensions enhance threading and conversation management capabilities further. Emerging enhancements include more sophisticated threading algorithms, adaptive conversation views tailored dynamically to user preferences or usage contexts, improved management of conversation metadata, and optimized handling of extensive or deeply nested conversational threads. These ongoing improvements ensure IMAP threading remains responsive, scalable, and highly effective in addressing evolving communication complexities characteristic of contemporary email interactions.

Email threading and conversation management within IMAP environments fundamentally transform email interactions, significantly improving comprehension, productivity, organization, collaborative efficiency, mobile usability, compliance management, and server performance. By enabling structured, coherent conversation views and efficient thread management functionalities, IMAP threading significantly enhances the email management experience, meeting critical communication demands in contemporary digital environments.

Handling Large Mailboxes

Managing large mailboxes efficiently is one of the most significant challenges facing users and administrators within IMAP (Internet Message Access Protocol) environments. As digital communication continues to expand rapidly, email inboxes can easily accumulate thousands, or even tens of thousands, of messages and attachments. Without effective management strategies, this growth leads to decreased performance, reduced responsiveness, difficulties in finding important emails, and potentially serious issues related to storage capacity and data management. IMAP provides robust tools, strategies, and mechanisms specifically designed to manage and optimize large mailboxes, ensuring email systems remain responsive, efficient, and user-friendly despite ever-growing volumes of stored information.

A core strategy for handling large mailboxes effectively involves intelligent mailbox structuring and folder hierarchy management. IMAP enables users to create elaborate, hierarchical folder systems on the server, organizing emails logically according to projects, topics, sender addresses, date ranges, or other personalized criteria. By actively structuring emails into appropriate folders and subfolders, users significantly enhance mailbox organization and clarity. A carefully managed hierarchical structure allows quick, intuitive navigation, simplifying email retrieval and dramatically improving productivity, even in mailboxes containing thousands of messages.

Another essential method for efficiently managing large mailboxes involves regular email archiving. IMAP supports systematic archiving strategies, allowing users or administrators to periodically move older or infrequently accessed messages from primary inboxes into dedicated archive folders. Archiving reduces inbox clutter, enhances responsiveness, and significantly accelerates synchronization times by minimizing the volume of messages clients must handle actively. Organizations frequently implement automated archival policies integrated with IMAP servers, moving messages automatically to archive locations based on defined age criteria or mailbox size thresholds. Regular archiving ensures inboxes remain manageable and highly performant, despite continuous email growth.

Search and filtering capabilities within IMAP servers also play crucial roles in effectively managing large mailboxes. Users frequently face difficulties locating specific messages within extensive email repositories, particularly when mailbox contents span multiple years or numerous communication threads. IMAP provides sophisticated server-side searching capabilities, enabling users to execute precise searches based on senders, recipients, subjects, dates, keywords, attachments, or message flags. Server-side searching eliminates the need for clients to download full mailbox content before executing searches, significantly improving search efficiency, responsiveness, and performance, particularly valuable when managing extensive mailboxes.

Similarly, IMAP-compatible email clients typically support robust filtering mechanisms, enabling users to define precise rules that automatically organize incoming messages into designated folders. Automated filtering significantly reduces manual organization tasks, minimizes inbox clutter, and ensures users maintain control over mailbox growth and complexity. Users can easily route lower-priority communications, newsletters, automated notifications, or marketing emails into dedicated folders, preserving inboxes primarily for essential or actionable communications. Intelligent filtering and automated categorization significantly improve mailbox management efficiency, responsiveness, and usability, especially in mailboxes receiving high volumes of daily messages.

Performance optimization strategies are critical for IMAP servers managing large mailbox environments. IMAP servers frequently implement sophisticated indexing solutions, maintaining structured indexes of message metadata, flags, headers, and attributes, enabling rapid message retrieval and responsive mailbox operations. High-performance indexing reduces latency and significantly accelerates synchronization, searching, and filtering processes, ensuring users experience smooth, efficient interactions with large mailboxes. Regular index optimization, database management, and performance monitoring activities are essential administrative tasks, proactively addressing performance bottlenecks and ensuring continuous optimization, responsiveness, and scalability.

Selective or partial synchronization is another valuable IMAP capability addressing large mailbox management challenges. Synchronizing complete mailbox content can become resource-intensive, slow, and bandwidth-consuming, particularly problematic for mobile clients or users accessing emails remotely. IMAP enables selective synchronization, allowing clients to download only recent messages, specific folders, headers, or message subsets matching defined criteria. Selective synchronization significantly reduces data transfers, enhances synchronization speeds, and optimizes bandwidth usage, providing efficient, responsive mailbox access even within extensive repositories.

IMAP compression provides additional performance optimization benefits for large mailbox environments. Compression algorithms effectively reduce data sizes transmitted between IMAP clients and servers, minimizing bandwidth usage, accelerating synchronization, and enhancing responsiveness. Compression is especially beneficial when users retrieve large numbers of messages simultaneously or manage substantial attachments frequently encountered in large mailboxes. Reduced data transfer sizes significantly enhance usability and responsiveness, particularly critical for mobile users or bandwidth-constrained environments.

Attachment management strategies contribute further to efficient large mailbox handling. Attachments frequently constitute significant portions of mailbox storage utilization, particularly when users exchange multimedia files, large documents, or graphics-intensive presentations regularly. Administrators commonly implement storage optimization strategies involving automated attachment archiving, compression, or dedicated attachment storage solutions, ensuring attachment storage remains efficient and manageable. Users benefit from responsive attachment retrieval, efficient mailbox storage utilization, and reduced synchronization overhead associated with managing extensive attachments.

Security considerations are integral in managing large mailboxes effectively. Extensive email repositories frequently include sensitive, confidential, or regulated information, requiring robust security measures protecting data integrity and confidentiality. Administrators implement comprehensive access controls, encryption standards, and intrusion prevention mechanisms to secure large mailbox environments. Access control lists (ACLs) enforce granular permissions, ensuring mailbox access remains restricted appropriately. Encrypted IMAP communications safeguard data during synchronization or mailbox interactions, preventing unauthorized data access or interception attempts. Comprehensive security strategies ensure large mailbox environments remain protected, secure, and compliant with organizational security policies or regulatory requirements.

Administrative oversight and user education significantly enhance large mailbox management effectiveness. Administrators regularly monitor mailbox sizes, growth trends, performance indicators, and synchronization behaviors, proactively identifying and addressing potential management challenges. Regular monitoring informs effective decision-making, supports strategic mailbox management policies, and enables continuous optimization of server performance, storage utilization, and resource allocation. Concurrently, user education ensures individuals understand best practices for efficient mailbox management, including archiving strategies, folder organization, filtering capabilities, and attachment handling methods, empowering users to actively manage mailbox complexity proactively and efficiently.

Continuous innovation in IMAP protocol extensions further enhances large mailbox management capabilities. Emerging extensions provide advanced functionalities such as adaptive synchronization, enhanced indexing strategies, improved compression mechanisms, and sophisticated mailbox analytics, proactively addressing evolving management challenges. Ongoing developments ensure IMAP continues delivering scalable, responsive, and highly effective solutions, enabling efficient large mailbox management in contemporary digital communication environments.

Efficiently handling large mailboxes within IMAP environments involves intelligent mailbox structuring, systematic archiving strategies, advanced searching and filtering capabilities, performance optimization techniques, selective synchronization, attachment management, security considerations, proactive administration, user education, and continuous protocol innovation, collectively ensuring email systems remain manageable, responsive, efficient, and secure, despite continually expanding volumes of digital communication.

Migration from Legacy Protocols to IMAP

Migrating from legacy email protocols, such as POP3 or earlier proprietary systems, to IMAP (Internet Message Access Protocol) represents an essential evolution for organizations and individuals seeking improved flexibility, synchronization, and advanced email management capabilities. Legacy protocols, designed in the early era of internet communication, often fail to meet contemporary demands for real-time synchronization, centralized storage, robust folder management, and efficient mailbox access across multiple devices. IMAP, specifically developed to address these limitations, offers powerful tools and features that significantly enhance the email experience, productivity, and overall management efficiency.

One of the primary motivations behind migrating from legacy protocols to IMAP involves overcoming the limitations inherent in POP3. The POP3 protocol, widely adopted historically due to its simplicity and early availability, primarily supports one-way message downloads from server to client. Once messages are retrieved by the client, they are often deleted from the server, leaving emails exclusively stored locally on individual devices. This model creates significant challenges, particularly when users access their email from multiple devices, locations, or clients. Without synchronization capabilities, POP3 users frequently experience inconsistencies, message duplication, lost emails, or confusion about message statuses, significantly diminishing email efficiency and usability.

IMAP directly addresses these challenges through its sophisticated synchronization and centralized storage mechanisms. Unlike POP3, IMAP maintains emails and mailbox data centrally on the server, ensuring continuous and consistent synchronization across multiple clients and devices. Actions performed on one device, such as reading, deleting, flagging, or moving messages, immediately synchronize with the IMAP server, reflecting changes instantly across all connected devices. Users benefit significantly from uniform mailbox views, consistent message states, and seamless email interactions, dramatically improving productivity, organization, and overall satisfaction with email management.

Migrating to IMAP also facilitates enhanced mailbox management and organization compared to legacy protocols. IMAP supports advanced hierarchical folder structures directly managed on servers, enabling logical, flexible email categorization and storage. Users migrating from POP3 often previously managed folders only locally within individual email clients, resulting in fragmented and inconsistent mailbox organization across multiple devices. IMAP ensures folder hierarchies remain consistently synchronized across all devices, allowing users to organize, access, and manage emails efficiently, regardless of which client or device they utilize. Centralized folder management significantly enhances mailbox organization, searchability, and productivity, particularly beneficial within organizational or collaborative environments.

Another critical benefit of migrating to IMAP involves improved backup, data protection, and disaster recovery capabilities. Legacy protocols relying exclusively on local message storage create substantial vulnerabilities related to data loss, corruption, or hardware failures. Users risk losing entire email repositories if local devices experience failures, malware infections, or accidental data deletions. IMAP's centralized storage model significantly simplifies comprehensive mailbox backup and recovery processes, ensuring email data remains consistently protected. Administrators implementing IMAP maintain regular, automated server backups, facilitating efficient disaster recovery and rapid mailbox restoration if incidents occur, providing significant reliability, peace of mind, and organizational resilience.

Successful migration from legacy protocols to IMAP requires careful planning, preparation, and execution to ensure smooth, efficient transitions with minimal disruptions. A well-executed migration typically involves detailed assessments of existing mailbox data, client configurations, user workflows, and organizational requirements. Administrators must evaluate existing mailbox volumes, attachment storage needs, folder structures, and user-specific preferences, carefully planning migration processes to ensure complete, accurate transfer of email messages, folders, attributes, and attachments from legacy systems to IMAP environments.

Administrators often leverage specialized migration tools designed explicitly for seamless legacy-to-IMAP transitions. Migration tools automate message transfers, folder mappings, metadata preservation, and synchronization processes, ensuring accurate replication of existing mailbox content within new IMAP environments. Advanced migration tools also provide comprehensive logging, detailed migration reports, and integrity verification, enabling administrators to closely monitor migration progress, detect issues proactively, and ensure comprehensive data integrity throughout the migration process.

User education and effective communication are essential components of successful IMAP migration projects. Users accustomed to legacy protocols frequently require guidance regarding IMAP's capabilities, synchronization mechanisms, folder management, and mailbox behaviors. Administrators conduct user training sessions, distribute comprehensive documentation, and provide personalized support, ensuring users understand IMAP's advantages, practical implications, and best practices. Effective user education ensures rapid user adoption, minimizes confusion, enhances productivity, and reduces support burdens during and after migration.

Performance considerations also play vital roles in legacy-to-IMAP migration processes. Organizations migrating extensive mailboxes, large attachment volumes, or numerous user accounts must proactively address potential performance bottlenecks or synchronization delays during migrations. Administrators frequently schedule migrations during off-peak periods or weekends, minimizing user disruptions and ensuring migration activities avoid negatively impacting ongoing organizational operations. Strategic migration scheduling ensures smooth performance, optimized bandwidth utilization, and efficient resource allocation throughout migration processes.

Security considerations remain integral throughout migration from legacy protocols to IMAP environments. Email data frequently contains sensitive, confidential, or regulated information requiring robust protection against unauthorized access, data breaches, or interception attempts during migration processes. Administrators ensure migration tools and processes utilize secure, encrypted communication channels, maintaining data integrity and confidentiality during transfers. Comprehensive access controls, encryption standards, and proactive security monitoring further safeguard email environments post-migration, ensuring IMAP implementations remain secure, compliant, and aligned with organizational security policies or regulatory requirements.

Migrating to IMAP provides significant scalability advantages compared to legacy protocols. Organizations experiencing continuous email growth require scalable solutions capable of efficiently managing expanding email repositories, attachment volumes, and user populations. IMAP's centralized storage, optimized indexing, efficient synchronization, and sophisticated folder management capabilities collectively enable significant scalability, allowing email infrastructures to efficiently accommodate future organizational growth without performance degradation, increased complexity, or resource inefficiencies.

Continuous advancements in IMAP protocol extensions further enhance migration processes, providing advanced capabilities such as improved synchronization performance, sophisticated mailbox management features, optimized attachment handling, and intelligent migration analytics. Protocol innovation ensures IMAP remains responsive, scalable, and highly adaptable, efficiently addressing emerging migration requirements, technological developments, and contemporary digital communication complexities.

Migration from legacy protocols to IMAP represents a strategic evolution significantly enhancing email synchronization, mailbox management, data protection, scalability, security, and overall productivity. Comprehensive migration planning, effective user education, strategic performance management, robust security practices, and continuous protocol innovation collectively ensure successful, efficient transitions to IMAP environments, enabling organizations and individuals to fully leverage IMAP's extensive email management capabilities in contemporary digital communication environments.

IMAP in Mobile Environments

The integration of IMAP within mobile environments has fundamentally reshaped how users interact with email, significantly enhancing mobility, accessibility, and real-time communication capabilities. As mobile devices such as smartphones and tablets have become integral parts of daily personal and professional life, demand for efficient and reliable mobile email management has grown exponentially. IMAP is uniquely suited to mobile environments due to its advanced synchronization capabilities, real-time notification support, efficient bandwidth usage, and optimized data transfer methods. These features ensure consistent, responsive, and seamless email access, even under challenging mobile network conditions.

One of the key strengths of IMAP within mobile environments is its inherent ability to provide real-time synchronization across multiple devices. IMAP maintains email data centrally on servers, meaning users who access their inbox through mobile devices always view the latest mailbox state. When actions such

IMAP and Cloud Integration

Integration of IMAP with cloud-based platforms has transformed the landscape of email management, providing unprecedented levels of flexibility, scalability, and accessibility. Cloud integration leverages IMAP's robust synchronization features, centralized storage, and seamless interoperability, allowing users and organizations to manage emails efficiently across multiple devices and platforms, without being constrained by geographical or hardware limitations. The widespread adoption of cloud solutions has fundamentally changed expectations around email availability, reliability, and collaboration, and IMAP plays a critical role in enabling these modern digital communication workflows.

IMAP's centralized server-based architecture aligns naturally with cloud storage models. By maintaining emails and mailbox metadata centrally in the cloud, IMAP ensures users have consistent and synchronized mailbox views, irrespective of their location or the specific device used to access their inbox. When users interact with their emails—such as reading messages, deleting items, or organizing folders—these changes immediately synchronize to cloud servers and become instantly available across other connected devices. This cloud-driven synchronization eliminates the complexity and inefficiency associated with traditional, locally stored email systems, delivering significant productivity and usability improvements.

Cloud-based IMAP implementations offer substantial scalability advantages compared to traditional on-premises solutions. As organizations experience growing email volumes, increasing numbers of users, and expanding storage requirements, cloud integration provides flexible and adaptive infrastructure to manage these evolving demands efficiently. IMAP, when paired with cloud platforms, supports dynamic allocation of storage resources, automatic scaling of mailboxes, and optimized handling of attachment-heavy communications. Organizations no longer face significant constraints related to physical hardware limitations, instead benefiting from the cloud's elastic capacity, allowing effortless scaling of email storage, bandwidth, and computing resources according to real-time organizational needs.

Another fundamental advantage of IMAP cloud integration is enhanced reliability and redundancy. Cloud-based email systems typically implement redundant infrastructure distributed across multiple geographic locations, providing robust protection against server failures, network disruptions, or catastrophic incidents. IMAP servers running in cloud environments benefit from automatic failover mechanisms, continuous data replication, and geographically dispersed data centers, ensuring continuous email availability and minimal downtime. Users can confidently rely on cloud-hosted IMAP email services for critical communications, benefiting from built-in redundancy and resilient infrastructure that safeguard email availability and accessibility, even in the event of local disruptions.

Integration of IMAP with cloud environments significantly simplifies backup, archival, and disaster recovery processes. Centralized cloud storage enables comprehensive and automated email backups, typically configured to capture mailbox snapshots at frequent intervals. These backups ensure email data remains consistently protected, enabling rapid restoration of mailboxes, folders, messages, or attachments following incidents such as data corruption, accidental deletions, or cybersecurity breaches. Cloud-based archival solutions seamlessly integrate with IMAP, systematically preserving email communications in compliance with organizational policies, regulatory requirements, or legal obligations. Efficient backup and archival capabilities deliver substantial peace of mind, data security, and compliance management advantages, essential components in contemporary digital communication environments.

Cloud-based IMAP solutions greatly enhance collaboration capabilities, particularly within organizational contexts. Modern cloud platforms frequently integrate IMAP services with collaborative tools such as calendars, contacts management, document sharing, task management, or instant messaging. Seamless integration allows users to easily coordinate email communications with related collaboration activities, improving productivity, workflow efficiency, and team coordination. IMAP synchronization ensures users across collaborative teams consistently access the latest email conversations, shared mailbox contents, or project-related communications, providing comprehensive visibility and facilitating streamlined collaborative interactions across dispersed teams or remote workers.

Performance optimization constitutes a key consideration within cloud-based IMAP deployments. Cloud infrastructure providers typically implement sophisticated performance optimization mechanisms, such as optimized indexing, caching strategies, load balancing, and dynamic resource allocation, ensuring IMAP services remain responsive and efficient, even under heavy usage or large-scale deployments. Optimized indexing accelerates email retrieval, folder operations, and synchronization responsiveness, ensuring users consistently experience smooth, high-performance email interactions. Load balancing evenly distributes client connections across multiple cloud servers, preventing performance bottlenecks, reducing latency, and maintaining efficient resource utilization within IMAP environments.

Security remains paramount in cloud-integrated IMAP implementations. Cloud providers offer comprehensive security frameworks encompassing robust encryption standards, secure authentication methods, intrusion detection systems, and real-time threat monitoring. IMAP communication channels frequently leverage SSL/TLS encryption, protecting sensitive email content and metadata during transmission between clients and cloud-based servers. Authentication methods such as OAuth2 or multi-factor authentication provide additional security layers, ensuring only authorized individuals access cloud-hosted mailboxes. Cloud security frameworks further encompass granular access control policies, comprehensive logging, and security audits, ensuring continuous protection against evolving cybersecurity threats, unauthorized access attempts, or data breaches.

Administrative oversight and streamlined management capabilities represent additional advantages within cloud-integrated IMAP environments. Cloud providers typically deliver intuitive administrative interfaces, centralized management dashboards, and comprehensive reporting functionalities, significantly simplifying email management tasks, resource monitoring, and system optimization. Administrators benefit from automated provisioning, streamlined user management, detailed mailbox analytics, and proactive alerts, enabling efficient management of IMAP services, mailbox quotas, storage utilization, and compliance requirements across organizational user populations. Streamlined administration reduces complexity, optimizes resource allocation, and improves overall efficiency within cloud-based IMAP deployments.

Cloud-based IMAP solutions offer significant cost efficiencies compared to traditional email infrastructure investments. Organizations leveraging cloud-integrated IMAP benefit from reduced upfront hardware costs, optimized infrastructure utilization, predictable operating expenses, and minimized administrative overhead. Cloud providers typically adopt subscription-based or usage-based pricing models, aligning IMAP service costs precisely with organizational requirements, mailbox capacities, and resource usage. Predictable, scalable pricing enables organizations to manage email expenditures effectively, efficiently allocate budgets, and optimize overall communication investments, delivering substantial financial advantages and long-term cost-efficiency improvements.

Continuous innovation within cloud platforms and ongoing IMAP protocol advancements ensure cloud-integrated IMAP solutions remain responsive, adaptive, and capable of addressing emerging communication demands, user expectations, and technological developments. Emerging innovations include advanced machine learning-based email categorization, predictive analytics, intelligent attachment management, enhanced mobile synchronization, and optimized cloud-to-device synchronization algorithms. These developments continually reinforce IMAP's central role in modern cloud-based communication environments, enabling highly effective, scalable, secure, and efficient email management capabilities.

Integration of IMAP within cloud environments profoundly transforms email communication, offering enhanced flexibility, centralized synchronization, scalability, reliability, collaboration capabilities, security protections, streamlined administration, cost efficiencies, and continuous innovation. These combined capabilities position cloud-integrated IMAP solutions as essential components enabling contemporary, productive, and efficient digital communication practices.

Troubleshooting Common IMAP Issues

Troubleshooting common IMAP issues requires a systematic approach to identify, diagnose, and resolve problems affecting email access, synchronization, or performance. IMAP, despite its advanced capabilities and robustness, occasionally presents challenges stemming from connectivity, authentication, mailbox synchronization, or server-related factors. Understanding how these issues manifest, recognizing symptoms, and employing effective resolution strategies ensures optimal email performance and minimizes disruption to users' communication workflows.

One common IMAP-related issue is authentication failure, often caused by incorrect login credentials, misconfigured client settings, or server-side authentication problems. Users typically encounter authentication errors when attempting to connect their email clients to IMAP servers. Initially, administrators should verify that users have entered accurate usernames, passwords, and server addresses. Additionally, reviewing server authentication logs may reveal precise error messages indicating incorrect credentials or failed login attempts. Resetting passwords, verifying account status, or reconfiguring client authentication settings can promptly resolve most authentication-related problems, restoring reliable email access.

Another frequent challenge involves mailbox synchronization inconsistencies. Users sometimes experience discrepancies between email states across multiple devices, manifesting as missing messages, unread emails appearing as read, or deleted emails persisting in client inboxes. Such synchronization issues frequently arise from improper client configuration, unstable network connections, or miscommunication between clients and IMAP servers. Administrators can resolve synchronization discrepancies by instructing users to refresh or resynchronize mailbox data. In persistent cases, resetting IMAP synchronization caches, recreating mail profiles, or adjusting synchronization intervals may prove necessary to restore mailbox consistency across devices.

Performance degradation represents another prevalent IMAP problem, commonly observed through slow email retrieval, delayed synchronization, or sluggish mailbox navigation. Performance issues typically result from overloaded IMAP servers, inefficient mailbox indexing, excessive mailbox sizes, or network latency. Administrators addressing performance concerns should first examine server resource utilization, monitoring CPU, memory, and disk usage to detect bottlenecks. Enhancing mailbox indexing, implementing server-side caching, optimizing client synchronization settings, and encouraging users to archive or delete unnecessary emails significantly improve performance responsiveness and mailbox efficiency.

Connectivity disruptions frequently hinder users' ability to access IMAP mailboxes consistently. Symptoms typically include timeouts, connection errors, or repeated reconnection attempts. Network-related factors, such as firewall restrictions, blocked IMAP ports, or unstable internet connectivity, commonly cause connectivity disruptions. Administrators should first validate network configurations, verifying firewall settings and ensuring necessary IMAP ports (such as ports 143 or 993) remain open and properly routed. Reviewing network logs and performing connectivity tests using diagnostic tools can pinpoint precise network obstacles. Resolving connectivity disruptions may involve modifying firewall rules, adjusting port-forwarding configurations, or improving overall network stability to maintain reliable IMAP connections.

Attachment handling issues occasionally arise, particularly involving large attachments or MIME type mismatches. Users may report difficulties downloading attachments, corrupt file downloads, or incorrect file type recognition. Attachment issues frequently result from client-side MIME misinterpretations, attachment size restrictions configured on servers, or corrupted email data. Troubleshooting attachment problems requires reviewing server attachment policies, analyzing MIME headers within problematic emails, and verifying attachment integrity through direct server-side downloads. Adjusting server attachment limits, reconfiguring client MIME type handling, or removing corrupted emails typically resolves attachment handling difficulties.

IMAP quota-related problems also occur regularly, notably when mailbox storage limits are exceeded. Users experiencing quota issues typically receive mailbox full notifications, email delivery rejections, or inability to store sent items. Administrators must review server storage quotas, examining mailbox utilization reports to identify users approaching or exceeding limits. Resolving quota-related issues involves instructing users to archive or delete older messages, increasing mailbox storage quotas, or employing automated quota management policies preventing mailbox overflows proactively.

Folder hierarchy inconsistencies represent another frequent IMAP challenge, arising when folders or subfolders fail to display correctly across clients or become duplicated unexpectedly. These problems typically stem from misconfigured IMAP namespace settings or incompatible folder hierarchy conventions between different email clients. Troubleshooting folder inconsistencies requires reviewing server namespace configurations, examining client folder settings, and verifying proper adherence to IMAP standards. Adjusting namespace parameters, renaming inconsistent folders, or recreating problematic mailbox profiles typically resolves folder hierarchy discrepancies.

Interoperability issues among diverse IMAP clients occasionally complicate troubleshooting efforts, as varying client implementations interpret IMAP standards inconsistently. Users may encounter unusual behaviors, such as incorrect message statuses, incompatible flag handling, or unreliable synchronization when using different email clients simultaneously. Addressing interoperability problems involves standardizing supported email client software, configuring client-specific IMAP settings consistently, and educating users about best practices for using multiple clients cohesively. Maintaining standardized client configurations and regular client software updates significantly reduce interoperability complications.

Effective IMAP troubleshooting necessitates comprehensive logging and monitoring practices. IMAP servers should generate detailed logs capturing authentication attempts, connection events, synchronization activities, message transactions, and error conditions. Administrators utilizing log analysis tools rapidly identify IMAP-related errors, pinpoint underlying issues, and initiate targeted resolutions effectively. Combining proactive log monitoring with real-time alerts ensures administrators quickly detect emerging problems, respond promptly, and maintain continuous IMAP service reliability and responsiveness.

User education and proactive communication further enhance IMAP troubleshooting effectiveness. Providing users clear guidance regarding IMAP best practices, recommended email management strategies, and reporting procedures encourages active participation in issue identification and resolution processes. Regular communication about known issues, maintenance schedules, or ongoing troubleshooting activities fosters user trust, improves issue reporting accuracy, and reduces frustration during troubleshooting efforts.

Logging and Monitoring in IMAP Servers

Logging and monitoring in IMAP servers play indispensable roles in ensuring optimal performance, security, and reliability within email management environments. Effective logging provides essential visibility into IMAP server operations, facilitating accurate diagnosis of issues, proactive detection of anomalies, and efficient resolution of problems. Comprehensive monitoring practices complement logging by continuously observing server resource utilization, email synchronization processes, connection stability, security events, and user activities, enabling administrators to maintain robust, secure, and efficient IMAP server infrastructures proactively.

IMAP servers generate diverse logs capturing detailed information about email-related events, authentication attempts, synchronization activities, mailbox transactions, and administrative actions. Authentication logs record successful and failed login attempts, identifying incorrect credentials, unauthorized access efforts, or suspicious authentication patterns. Synchronization logs document mailbox updates, client-server interactions, and synchronization errors, providing valuable insight into synchronization discrepancies or performance bottlenecks. Connection logs track network connections, timeouts, and errors, revealing connectivity disruptions or network-related obstacles hindering IMAP performance.

Monitoring IMAP server performance metrics is equally critical, enabling administrators to proactively identify resource constraints, scalability limitations, or infrastructure inefficiencies. Effective monitoring solutions observe essential performance indicators, such as CPU utilization, memory consumption, disk space availability, network bandwidth usage, mailbox access frequency, and concurrent client connections. Real-time monitoring dashboards provide administrators immediate visibility into server health, resource allocation, and operational performance, facilitating informed decision-making, proactive resource management, and continuous optimization of IMAP server environments.

Security-focused logging and monitoring significantly enhance IMAP server protection against unauthorized access, data breaches, or cybersecurity threats. Comprehensive security logs capture events such as suspicious login attempts, account lockouts, privilege escalations, data access anomalies, or configuration changes. Intrusion detection systems monitor network traffic, server interactions, and IMAP protocol behavior, immediately alerting administrators regarding potential security breaches, malicious activities, or unauthorized access attempts. Proactive security monitoring enables rapid identification, containment, and remediation of security incidents, maintaining email confidentiality, integrity, and compliance with organizational security standards or regulatory requirements.

Analyzing IMAP logs and monitoring data frequently involves utilizing specialized log analysis tools or monitoring platforms capable of parsing extensive log data, correlating related events, and providing actionable insights through comprehensive reports, visual dashboards, or alerting mechanisms.

Backup and Recovery Strategies

Backup and recovery strategies form a critical foundation within IMAP-based email environments, ensuring data integrity, continuity, and rapid restoration of email services following unexpected incidents or failures. Effective backup practices safeguard essential email communications, attachments, mailbox structures, and critical metadata against data loss, corruption, accidental deletions, malicious cyber-attacks, hardware failures, or natural disasters. Similarly, well-defined recovery strategies ensure prompt restoration of email access, minimize disruption to user workflows, and maintain organizational productivity, even when confronted with serious technical challenges or catastrophic events.

IMAP's inherent architecture, characterized by centralized email storage on servers, significantly facilitates efficient and comprehensive backup procedures. Centralization enables administrators to systematically capture complete mailbox snapshots, including message content, attachments, hierarchical folder structures, message flags, and associated metadata. Backing up entire mailboxes centrally ensures administrators maintain accurate, complete, and reliable email records that users can quickly recover or restore if data loss occurs.

Centralized storage streamlines backup processes, simplifying administrative management, reducing backup complexity, and significantly improving efficiency compared to decentralized email storage models.

A cornerstone of robust IMAP backup strategies involves implementing automated, scheduled backups at consistent intervals, frequently daily or even more regularly for highly active environments. Automated backups systematically capture incremental mailbox changes, ensuring backup copies remain consistently up-to-date with minimal data loss risks. Employing incremental or differential backup methodologies significantly enhances backup efficiency by capturing only mailbox changes occurring since the last successful backup. Incremental backups optimize backup storage usage, reduce network bandwidth consumption, and enable rapid completion of backup processes, especially beneficial when managing extensive mailbox repositories.

To further enhance data protection, many IMAP backup strategies involve storing multiple backup copies distributed across diverse storage locations or geographic sites. Distributing backups protects email data against localized failures, natural disasters, or cyber incidents impacting single storage locations. Administrators often leverage cloud-based backup solutions to achieve geographic redundancy, securely storing encrypted email backups in cloud data centers dispersed across multiple regions. Geographic distribution ensures email backups remain continuously accessible, resilient, and highly recoverable, regardless of localized incidents affecting primary server infrastructures.

Retention policies represent another critical consideration within IMAP backup strategies. Organizations frequently define specific retention periods, determining precisely how long backup copies remain stored before systematic purging occurs. Retention policies typically align with regulatory compliance requirements, organizational data management standards, or storage resource limitations. Implementing structured retention strategies ensures administrators balance email data recoverability needs effectively against storage resource optimization requirements, maintaining comprehensive yet efficient backup repositories that fully satisfy organizational retention obligations.

Backup security constitutes a vital component of comprehensive IMAP backup strategies. Email backups frequently contain sensitive, confidential, or regulated information, requiring stringent protection against unauthorized access, interception, or breaches. Administrators ensure backups employ robust encryption standards, securing email content and metadata during storage and transmission processes. Secure storage solutions, encrypted transmission channels, and comprehensive access control policies prevent unauthorized backup access or manipulation, safeguarding email backups against emerging cybersecurity threats, internal misuse, or regulatory compliance breaches.

Rapid recovery capabilities significantly influence the effectiveness of IMAP backup strategies, emphasizing streamlined restoration processes capable of promptly reinstating mailbox access and functionality. Administrators typically leverage specialized recovery tools or solutions facilitating efficient mailbox restoration, folder reconstruction, message recovery, or attachment retrieval from backup repositories. Effective recovery tools allow selective restoration, enabling administrators to recover specific mailbox subsets, particular email messages, individual folders, or even single attachments efficiently. Granular recovery capabilities significantly enhance recovery flexibility, reduce restoration complexity, and accelerate recovery timelines following email data loss incidents.

Comprehensive disaster recovery planning extends beyond standard backups, encompassing strategic processes, detailed procedures, and actionable plans enabling rapid restoration of complete IMAP infrastructures following severe incidents. Disaster recovery strategies typically define precise recovery point objectives (RPO) and recovery time objectives (RTO), establishing explicit parameters regarding acceptable data loss levels and maximum allowable restoration durations following disruptions. Clearly defined disaster recovery objectives ensure administrators proactively manage risks, strategically allocate resources, and establish effective recovery processes ensuring rapid resumption of email services even in catastrophic scenarios.

Administrators frequently conduct regular backup validation and recovery testing exercises, verifying backup integrity, assessing restoration reliability, and identifying potential weaknesses within backup or recovery procedures. Routine backup validation involves examining backup consistency, verifying mailbox data completeness, and detecting backup corruption proactively. Recovery testing exercises simulate realistic restoration scenarios, allowing administrators to evaluate recovery processes, validate RPO/RTO adherence, and optimize recovery methodologies continuously. Regular validation and testing activities ensure backup reliability, reinforce recovery preparedness, and enhance administrator confidence regarding email data recoverability.

Effective backup and recovery strategies within IMAP environments involve comprehensive documentation, clearly articulating backup schedules, retention policies, security measures, recovery procedures, disaster recovery plans, validation methodologies, and testing protocols. Comprehensive documentation provides administrators detailed guidelines ensuring consistent, reliable, and accurate backup or recovery actions, especially valuable during high-pressure recovery situations following data loss incidents. Documented procedures enhance administrative efficiency, reduce human errors, streamline recovery activities, and facilitate effective knowledge transfer among IT staff or recovery teams.

Continuous monitoring and reporting significantly improve backup reliability, enabling administrators to monitor backup status, detect backup failures proactively, identify performance bottlenecks, and ensure backup schedules remain consistently maintained. Monitoring solutions frequently provide automated alerts or notifications regarding backup anomalies, incomplete backups, or storage resource constraints, facilitating rapid administrative intervention and issue resolution. Regular backup reporting summarizes backup activities, verifies policy adherence, and provides valuable insights informing strategic backup improvements, storage resource optimization, or infrastructure investments.

Backup and recovery strategies within IMAP environments remain continuously adaptive, regularly incorporating technological advancements, emerging best practices, and evolving organizational requirements. Ongoing innovations introduce advanced backup methodologies, improved encryption standards, intelligent backup analytics, optimized recovery algorithms, or sophisticated disaster recovery automation tools. Continuous evolution ensures IMAP backup strategies remain responsive, effective, resilient, and scalable, proactively addressing contemporary data protection challenges, cybersecurity threats, and compliance obligations characteristic of modern digital communication environments.

Scaling IMAP Infrastructure

Scaling IMAP infrastructure effectively is a critical undertaking for organizations experiencing increased user populations, expanding mailbox sizes, higher email traffic volumes, or growing demands for real-time synchronization. As email communication becomes an increasingly central component of organizational operations, ensuring that IMAP infrastructures can efficiently accommodate growth without compromising performance, reliability, or responsiveness becomes paramount. Effective scaling involves strategic infrastructure planning, resource optimization, redundancy measures, performance tuning, and comprehensive management strategies, collectively enabling IMAP environments to remain robust and highly performant even under intense usage scenarios or rapid growth trajectories.

A fundamental aspect of scaling IMAP infrastructure involves enhancing server hardware resources strategically. IMAP servers require adequate processing power, sufficient memory, fast disk storage, and robust network connectivity to manage increased workloads effectively. Administrators must continuously assess current resource utilization trends, proactively identifying resource bottlenecks, capacity limitations, or potential performance degradation risks. Scaling hardware resources strategically, such as upgrading processors, increasing RAM capacities, implementing faster solid-state drives, or enhancing network bandwidth, significantly improves IMAP server performance, enabling efficient management of larger mailbox repositories, heavier synchronization workloads, and higher concurrent client connections.

Load balancing constitutes another essential strategy in scaling IMAP infrastructure efficiently. Load balancers distribute incoming IMAP client requests across multiple IMAP server instances, evenly spreading workloads, preventing individual server overloads, and maintaining responsive, reliable email services. Implementing load balancing ensures efficient utilization of available server resources, reducing latency, minimizing response times, and optimizing IMAP service availability under intensive usage conditions. Load balancing configurations frequently leverage advanced algorithms such as round-robin, least connections, or weighted distributions, strategically allocating client connections according to real-time server capacity, resource availability, or current workload distributions.

IMAP infrastructure scaling often involves adopting clustering or distributed architectures, enhancing reliability, redundancy, and scalability. Clustering multiple IMAP server nodes enables fault tolerance, automatic failover mechanisms, and seamless load distribution. Distributed architectures distribute mailbox storage across multiple nodes, allowing parallel processing of mailbox transactions, rapid message retrieval, and scalable storage capacities. Implementing clustered or distributed IMAP architectures significantly enhances service resilience, minimizing downtime, ensuring continuous email availability, and efficiently supporting growing user populations, mailbox sizes, and email traffic volumes.

Optimizing mailbox storage represents a crucial factor within scalable IMAP infrastructures. Effective storage optimization strategies involve implementing efficient indexing mechanisms, utilizing database-driven storage solutions, or employing advanced file systems optimized specifically for email storage workloads. Advanced indexing accelerates message retrieval, mailbox searching, folder synchronization, and metadata processing, dramatically improving IMAP server responsiveness and reducing latency. Administrators may additionally utilize storage tiering strategies, storing frequently accessed mailboxes on high-performance storage tiers while archiving older, infrequently accessed emails to cost-effective storage solutions, ensuring optimized storage resource utilization aligned precisely with mailbox access patterns and organizational requirements.

Strategically integrating caching mechanisms significantly enhances IMAP infrastructure scalability. IMAP servers frequently handle repetitive client requests, message retrieval operations, or metadata transactions. Implementing caching solutions at various infrastructure layers, including memory caches, file system caches, or distributed cache clusters, reduces redundant processing, minimizes disk I/O overhead, and accelerates response times significantly. Intelligent caching algorithms dynamically manage cached mailbox content, metadata, or client session information, ensuring rapid data retrieval, optimized synchronization performance, and efficient resource utilization within scalable IMAP environments.

Proactively managing IMAP client synchronization behaviors further supports scalable infrastructure performance. Email clients continuously synchronizing extensive mailbox repositories can significantly impact server workloads, resource consumption, and network utilization. Administrators strategically configure IMAP clients to optimize synchronization intervals, implement partial synchronization policies, limit client resource consumption, or selectively synchronize high-priority mailbox subsets. Effective synchronization management minimizes unnecessary resource overhead, optimizes synchronization performance, and ensures infrastructure resources efficiently accommodate increased user concurrency and mailbox volumes without experiencing performance degradation.

Monitoring and capacity planning activities represent essential practices within scalable IMAP infrastructure management. Comprehensive monitoring solutions continuously observe server resource utilization, mailbox storage trends, concurrent client connections, synchronization activities, and network bandwidth consumption. Detailed monitoring data informs strategic capacity planning decisions, enabling administrators to proactively allocate resources, anticipate growth trajectories, and prevent infrastructure constraints proactively. Regular capacity assessments facilitate informed hardware upgrades, storage expansions, bandwidth enhancements, or architectural adjustments, ensuring IMAP infrastructures remain continuously prepared for anticipated organizational growth scenarios.

Scalable IMAP infrastructures frequently incorporate cloud-based resources, leveraging cloud infrastructure providers' inherent scalability advantages. Cloud-based IMAP implementations dynamically allocate infrastructure resources according to real-time demands, enabling elastic scalability, adaptive storage capacities, and optimized resource provisioning aligned precisely with organizational requirements. Cloud infrastructure providers additionally deliver built-in redundancy, geographic distribution, load balancing capabilities, and performance optimization mechanisms, ensuring IMAP environments remain highly responsive, resilient, and scalable even within intensive usage scenarios or rapid growth contexts.

Security considerations remain integral within scalable IMAP infrastructure implementations, especially as user populations, mailbox repositories, and resource utilization expand significantly. Comprehensive security frameworks encompass robust encryption standards, secure authentication protocols, granular access control policies, and proactive threat monitoring mechanisms. Scaling IMAP infrastructures securely involves maintaining encrypted communication channels, enforcing authentication standards consistently, implementing detailed logging practices, and continuously monitoring security-related events proactively. Security frameworks ensure email confidentiality, data integrity, and regulatory compliance, effectively safeguarding scalable IMAP infrastructures against cybersecurity threats, unauthorized access attempts, or data breaches.

Administrative management strategies further support effective IMAP infrastructure scalability. Streamlined management solutions provide centralized administration interfaces, detailed performance analytics, automated provisioning capabilities, and comprehensive reporting functionalities. Centralized management reduces administrative complexity, simplifies infrastructure oversight, optimizes resource allocation, and enables administrators to efficiently manage extensive IMAP server deployments, large user populations, and continuously expanding mailbox repositories strategically and proactively.

Continuous protocol innovation and ongoing technological advancements ensure IMAP infrastructures remain highly scalable, responsive, and adaptive. Emerging IMAP protocol extensions introduce advanced synchronization algorithms, optimized indexing methodologies, improved caching strategies, intelligent storage management, and enhanced performance tuning capabilities. Continuous innovation ensures IMAP infrastructure scalability effectively addresses contemporary communication complexities, evolving user expectations, rapid organizational growth, and technological advancements characteristic of modern digital communication environments.

High Availability for IMAP Services

High availability is a critical aspect in the deployment and management of IMAP-based email infrastructures, directly impacting the reliability, responsiveness, and user satisfaction associated with email services. Ensuring high availability means designing IMAP systems that maintain uninterrupted accessibility, minimal downtime, and consistent performance even in the presence of hardware failures, network disruptions, software issues, or other unexpected incidents. As email communication becomes indispensable for organizations, achieving and sustaining high availability within IMAP environments requires strategic planning, resilient architecture design, redundancy implementation, continuous monitoring, proactive management, and robust recovery mechanisms.

A foundational element of high availability in IMAP services is infrastructure redundancy. Redundant architectures consist of multiple, simultaneously active IMAP server instances, ensuring no single point of failure exists within the infrastructure. Each server node independently maintains synchronization with shared mailbox storage, message repositories, and metadata. Redundancy enables automatic failover, seamless load balancing, and dynamic distribution of user requests across multiple servers. If one server experiences issues or becomes unavailable, redundant instances automatically take over affected workloads, ensuring uninterrupted IMAP service continuity, rapid recovery, and minimal service disruption experienced by end users.

Clustering represents a core redundancy strategy widely employed in achieving high availability within IMAP environments. Clustered IMAP server configurations group multiple server instances into cohesive clusters capable of automatically redistributing workloads, sharing mailbox access responsibilities, and collectively managing concurrent user connections. Clustered architectures often incorporate advanced cluster management solutions capable of dynamically monitoring server health, resource availability, network connectivity, and workload distribution in real time. Clustering ensures seamless failover among server nodes, immediately reallocating user connections, mailbox access, and synchronization requests if specific cluster nodes experience failure or performance degradation, significantly enhancing overall IMAP service resilience.

Geographic redundancy further enhances IMAP service availability, protecting infrastructures against localized incidents, environmental disasters, or data center outages. Geographic redundancy involves strategically distributing IMAP infrastructure components, mailbox storage repositories, and server clusters across multiple data centers situated in diverse geographic locations. Distributed geographic configurations enable automated failover processes to activate backup IMAP infrastructures located in unaffected data centers if primary infrastructures experience disruption or outages. Geographic redundancy ensures continuous mailbox access, uninterrupted email synchronization, and resilient infrastructure protection, even in catastrophic scenarios impacting entire data center locations.

Load balancing constitutes an essential high availability strategy, enabling efficient distribution of IMAP client requests across redundant server instances and clusters. Load balancers dynamically route user connections, mailbox synchronization requests, and message retrieval operations according to current server capacities, resource availability, and workload distribution. Effective load balancing significantly enhances IMAP infrastructure responsiveness, minimizes request latency, optimizes server utilization, and prevents performance bottlenecks under intensive usage conditions. Additionally, load balancers proactively monitor IMAP server health, resource consumption, and response times, automatically rerouting client requests if server nodes experience degraded performance or availability concerns.

Robust data replication methodologies play crucial roles in maintaining high availability within IMAP environments. Data replication continuously synchronizes mailbox contents, messages, attachments, metadata, and server configurations among redundant IMAP infrastructure components. Replication ensures mailbox data consistency, synchronization integrity, and reliable message accessibility across multiple server instances and geographic locations. Advanced replication solutions employ real-time or near-real-time synchronization processes, rapidly propagating mailbox changes, folder modifications, message additions, deletions, or flag status updates among redundant infrastructure nodes. Reliable replication guarantees consistent mailbox experiences, uninterrupted message availability, and immediate mailbox restoration during failover or recovery scenarios.

Advanced storage solutions significantly contribute to high availability strategies, providing resilient, fault-tolerant, and highly performant mailbox storage infrastructures. High-availability storage architectures commonly incorporate redundant storage arrays, clustered file systems, distributed database solutions, or cloud-based storage services explicitly optimized for email storage workloads. Storage solutions frequently implement RAID configurations, multi-node redundancy, real-time replication mechanisms, and automated failover processes, ensuring mailbox data remains continuously accessible, reliable, and recoverable despite storage hardware failures, disk corruption, or component outages. Robust storage infrastructures underpin overall IMAP availability, maintaining reliable mailbox access, consistent synchronization responsiveness, and data integrity.

Comprehensive monitoring and alerting mechanisms represent vital elements within high availability IMAP infrastructures, providing continuous visibility into server health, resource utilization, synchronization performance, connectivity status, and system events. Effective monitoring solutions observe critical IMAP service metrics, including server responsiveness, mailbox access latency, synchronization delays, network availability, and resource consumption. Real-time monitoring dashboards immediately identify potential availability concerns, automatically generating alerts notifying administrators of performance anomalies, connectivity disruptions, or infrastructure degradation. Proactive monitoring ensures administrators rapidly detect, diagnose, and address emerging availability issues, preventing extensive downtime and service disruption.

Rapid recovery capabilities remain integral within high availability IMAP environments, emphasizing streamlined recovery processes capable of promptly reinstating service functionality and mailbox accessibility following infrastructure disruptions or component failures. High availability recovery mechanisms often incorporate automated failover solutions, automated mailbox restoration capabilities, rapid infrastructure reprovisioning tools, and clearly documented recovery procedures. Efficient recovery tools allow administrators to swiftly recover mailbox access, reinstate synchronization processes, restore lost messages, or activate backup infrastructure nodes immediately upon incident detection. Prompt recovery capabilities significantly enhance IMAP service resilience, minimize downtime durations, and sustain continuous mailbox availability.

Security considerations remain essential when designing and managing high availability IMAP infrastructures. Comprehensive security frameworks encompass encrypted communication channels, secure authentication protocols, rigorous access control policies, proactive threat monitoring mechanisms, and resilient security infrastructures. Maintaining high availability securely involves ensuring encryption standards, authentication methods, access controls, and intrusion detection mechanisms remain consistently enforced across redundant infrastructure nodes. Robust security practices safeguard IMAP infrastructures against unauthorized access attempts, cyber-attacks, and data breaches, ensuring continuous protection and compliance with organizational security policies and regulatory requirements.

Continuous administrative oversight significantly supports high availability management within IMAP infrastructures. Streamlined management solutions provide centralized administration interfaces, detailed performance analytics, automated infrastructure provisioning capabilities, comprehensive reporting functionalities, and proactive alerting mechanisms. Centralized management enables administrators to efficiently monitor redundant infrastructure health, manage resource allocations dynamically, adjust failover policies strategically, and rapidly respond to emerging availability concerns. Effective administrative oversight ensures infrastructure resources remain optimized, highly available, resilient, and responsive, even within intensive usage scenarios or rapid organizational growth contexts.

Ongoing protocol innovations and technological advancements continually enhance high availability capabilities within IMAP environments. Emerging innovations introduce advanced clustering methodologies, intelligent replication algorithms, enhanced monitoring solutions, automated disaster recovery capabilities, resilient storage architectures, and optimized failover mechanisms. Continuous innovation ensures IMAP infrastructure availability remains responsive, effective, resilient, and highly adaptive, addressing evolving availability challenges, technological advancements, and contemporary digital communication complexities characteristic of modern organizational requirements.

IMAP Load Balancing Techniques

Load balancing is an essential technique within IMAP infrastructures, aimed at ensuring optimal performance, high availability, scalability, and reliability for email services. As email traffic and user demand increase, IMAP servers frequently face intense workloads, high concurrency rates, and extensive mailbox synchronization requests. Load balancing distributes incoming IMAP client requests evenly across multiple server instances, reducing the burden on individual servers, preventing performance bottlenecks, and maintaining consistent email responsiveness. Effective implementation of load balancing techniques ensures IMAP environments remain highly performant, responsive, and scalable, efficiently accommodating expanding user populations and growing email demands.

Several load balancing methodologies exist, each providing distinct advantages within IMAP deployments. The simplest method, known as round-robin load balancing, sequentially assigns client connections to available IMAP servers. This basic technique distributes workloads evenly among servers, effectively managing resource utilization.

Round-robin methods are straightforward, easily implemented, and suitable for environments with relatively uniform IMAP workloads and server capacities. However, the round-robin approach may become less effective if servers differ significantly in resource availability, processing power, or mailbox access workloads, as uneven resource usage can still occur.

To address this potential limitation, weighted round-robin load balancing introduces weight assignments reflecting individual server capacities, resource availability, or processing capabilities. Weighted distributions allocate client connections proportionally according to predefined server weights, ensuring more powerful or resource-rich servers receive correspondingly higher client workloads. Administrators can dynamically adjust server weights based on performance trends, hardware upgrades, or resource utilization patterns, continuously optimizing load distribution efficiency. Weighted round-robin methodologies significantly enhance resource allocation precision, workload balance accuracy, and overall IMAP infrastructure responsiveness compared to basic round-robin methods.

Least connections load balancing represents another highly effective methodology, dynamically distributing client requests according to real-time server connection counts. This method routes incoming IMAP requests to the server currently handling the fewest active client connections, proactively balancing workloads based directly on instantaneous server utilization metrics. Least connections methodologies rapidly respond to changing workload distributions, automatically compensating for servers becoming overloaded or experiencing resource constraints. Particularly beneficial in highly dynamic IMAP environments, least connections approaches efficiently maintain workload balance, minimize latency, and optimize server responsiveness even under intense usage conditions.

IP hash load balancing offers another valuable technique, consistently directing client connections to specific IMAP servers based upon client IP addresses. By employing hashing algorithms applied to client IP information, IP hash methods consistently route individual client connections to the same IMAP server across multiple sessions. Consistent server assignment provides valuable benefits, including optimized mailbox synchronization performance, reduced mailbox state inconsistencies, and efficient server-side caching utilization. IP hash load balancing effectively supports environments where consistent client-server sessions are desirable, significantly enhancing synchronization reliability, performance responsiveness, and user experience consistency.

Advanced IMAP load balancing solutions frequently combine multiple methodologies, employing hybrid approaches dynamically adapting to varying infrastructure conditions, usage patterns, or client requirements. Hybrid load balancing mechanisms intelligently evaluate multiple factors, including server health metrics, response times, resource availability, current connection loads, and client attributes, strategically allocating incoming IMAP requests accordingly. Intelligent hybrid approaches maximize load balancing efficiency, performance optimization precision, infrastructure resource utilization effectiveness, and IMAP service reliability within complex, large-scale deployment scenarios.

Effective load balancing involves implementing robust health check mechanisms continually monitoring IMAP server status, resource utilization, mailbox synchronization responsiveness, and infrastructure availability. Load balancers regularly perform proactive health checks, rapidly identifying server nodes experiencing degraded performance, connection disruptions, or resource exhaustion conditions. Upon detecting compromised server health, load balancers automatically reroute incoming IMAP requests away from affected servers, reallocating workloads across remaining healthy server instances dynamically. Health check methodologies significantly enhance infrastructure resilience, availability continuity, proactive performance management, and rapid recovery capabilities following server disruptions or outages.

Geographically distributed IMAP deployments frequently employ global load balancing techniques, strategically distributing client connections across geographically dispersed data centers or server clusters. Global load balancers dynamically evaluate factors such as client location, network latency, data center capacity, infrastructure availability, and server responsiveness, optimally routing IMAP client connections to geographically advantageous infrastructure components. Global load balancing ensures optimal synchronization performance, minimal latency, efficient resource utilization, and resilient infrastructure redundancy across multiple geographic locations, significantly enhancing IMAP service reliability, responsiveness, and geographic scalability.

Effective IMAP load balancing implementations leverage dedicated load balancing hardware appliances or software solutions explicitly optimized for email protocols and IMAP workloads. Hardware load balancers frequently deliver high throughput capabilities, low-latency performance, advanced algorithm support, comprehensive monitoring functionalities, and robust failover mechanisms, efficiently supporting intensive IMAP usage scenarios. Software-based load balancers typically provide flexible deployment options, simplified configuration interfaces, comprehensive analytics, and extensive integration capabilities within virtualized environments or cloud-based IMAP deployments. Administrators strategically select appropriate load balancing solutions aligning precisely with organizational performance requirements, scalability objectives, infrastructure configurations, and budget considerations.

Security considerations remain integral within effective IMAP load balancing strategies. Comprehensive security practices involve ensuring encrypted communication channels between clients, load balancers, and IMAP servers, preventing unauthorized access, data interception, or communication breaches. Load balancers frequently incorporate SSL/TLS encryption offloading functionalities, efficiently managing encryption overhead while securely transmitting IMAP traffic between client endpoints and backend server infrastructure. Robust access control policies, secure authentication methodologies, intrusion detection systems, and proactive threat monitoring mechanisms ensure load balancing infrastructures remain continuously protected against emerging cybersecurity threats, unauthorized access attempts, or malicious activities.

Administrative oversight significantly enhances load balancing efficiency within IMAP environments. Streamlined management solutions deliver centralized configuration interfaces, detailed performance analytics, comprehensive reporting functionalities, automated provisioning capabilities, and proactive alerting mechanisms. Centralized administration simplifies load balancer configuration management, performance tuning, resource allocation adjustments, and infrastructure monitoring tasks. Effective administrative management ensures load balancing solutions remain continuously optimized, highly responsive, resilient, and adaptable, efficiently supporting evolving organizational requirements, IMAP workloads, and scalability objectives.

Continuous protocol innovation and technological advancements ensure IMAP load balancing techniques remain responsive, scalable, and adaptive. Emerging innovations introduce advanced algorithm support, intelligent client request routing methodologies, enhanced health monitoring capabilities, optimized geographic load distribution mechanisms, and resilient redundancy functionalities. Continuous evolution ensures IMAP load balancing remains capable of addressing contemporary infrastructure complexities, dynamic workload distributions, growing email demands, technological developments, and evolving digital communication environments characteristic of modern organizational deployments.

Email Archiving with IMAP

Email archiving within IMAP-based environments plays a fundamental role in managing email efficiently, safeguarding critical communication, complying with regulatory requirements, and optimizing mailbox performance. As organizations and individuals experience exponential growth in email traffic and mailbox volumes, effective archiving solutions become essential for maintaining streamlined inboxes, enhancing search capabilities, and preserving historical email data securely. IMAP's intrinsic capabilities for centralized storage, hierarchical mailbox structures, server-based synchronization, and flexible access provide an ideal foundation upon which robust archiving strategies can be developed, integrated, and maintained effectively.

Archiving emails using IMAP enables organizations to systematically move older or infrequently accessed messages from primary inboxes to dedicated archive folders located directly on the server. Unlike traditional client-side archiving solutions that store archived messages locally on individual devices, IMAP server-based archiving centralizes storage, ensuring archived emails remain consistently accessible, synchronized, and retrievable across multiple devices and email clients. Centralized archiving solutions ensure archived emails are protected against data loss resulting from local device failures, hardware corruption, accidental deletions, or malware infections, significantly enhancing email data security, reliability, and continuity.

IMAP's hierarchical folder structures greatly facilitate systematic and organized email archiving. Users or administrators typically create dedicated archive folders and subfolders categorized according to specific criteria, such as date ranges, projects, departments, sender addresses, or compliance requirements. Emails are periodically or automatically relocated from primary mailbox folders into these structured archive folders, significantly reducing inbox clutter, streamlining mailbox organization, and enhancing email retrieval efficiency. Hierarchical archive structures simplify message retrieval processes, enabling users to quickly locate specific archived messages through intuitive folder navigation, improving productivity, workflow efficiency, and organizational clarity.

Automated archiving methodologies commonly integrated within IMAP servers significantly enhance archiving efficiency and consistency. Automated archiving processes proactively monitor mailbox content, periodically evaluating messages based upon predefined criteria such as message age, mailbox quotas, or message read status. When defined archiving thresholds are met, automated systems automatically relocate identified emails from inbox folders into appropriate archive locations, reducing manual workload burdens and ensuring email archiving consistently adheres to organizational policies or regulatory compliance mandates. Automation significantly improves archiving accuracy, reduces human error risks, optimizes storage resource utilization, and maintains streamlined, manageable inboxes proactively.

Compliance management constitutes a critical objective within email archiving strategies, particularly within regulated industries subject to stringent legal, financial, or governmental oversight. Regulatory frameworks frequently mandate retention of email communications for defined periods, requiring organizations to implement comprehensive archiving solutions ensuring email preservation, retrievability, and auditability according to precise regulatory specifications. IMAP server-based archiving effectively supports compliance management through systematic email retention, secure storage methodologies, robust indexing capabilities, and efficient retrieval mechanisms. Compliance-oriented archiving solutions incorporate detailed indexing of email metadata, content, attachments, sender information, recipient details, and timestamps, ensuring archived emails remain easily searchable, verifiable, and retrievable during compliance audits, legal discovery processes, or internal investigations.

Advanced IMAP archiving solutions frequently integrate comprehensive search capabilities, enabling users or compliance officers to rapidly locate archived emails based upon diverse criteria such as sender addresses, recipients, subject lines, date ranges, keywords, attachment presence, or message attributes. Robust server-side indexing solutions accelerate archived email retrieval, significantly reducing search latency, minimizing response times, and enhancing search precision within extensive archival repositories containing thousands or even millions of messages. Efficient search functionalities improve productivity, facilitate timely compliance responses, and optimize historical email data accessibility within complex, large-scale archiving deployments.

Optimizing storage resource utilization represents another key consideration within IMAP email archiving strategies. Archived emails frequently represent substantial storage resource consumption, particularly within organizations maintaining extensive historical email repositories or managing significant attachment volumes. Effective storage optimization strategies involve employing data compression methodologies, deduplication technologies, attachment management solutions, or storage tiering strategies, strategically managing archived email storage resources to maximize efficiency, scalability, and cost-effectiveness. Storage tiering involves storing recent or frequently accessed archived emails on high-performance storage tiers while relocating older, infrequently accessed messages to cost-effective storage solutions, ensuring optimized storage utilization precisely aligned with organizational email access patterns and archival objectives.

Security considerations remain integral within effective IMAP email archiving implementations. Archived emails regularly contain sensitive, confidential, proprietary, or regulated information necessitating robust protection against unauthorized access, interception, breaches, or internal misuse. Comprehensive security frameworks employ robust encryption methodologies securing archived email content and metadata both during storage and throughout transmission processes. Encrypted storage solutions, secure communication channels, comprehensive access control policies, multi-factor authentication methods, and proactive threat monitoring mechanisms collectively safeguard archived emails effectively, ensuring confidentiality, data integrity, and continuous compliance with stringent organizational security policies or regulatory requirements.

Efficient email archiving within IMAP environments significantly enhances mailbox performance and synchronization responsiveness. Active mailboxes containing extensive message volumes often experience sluggish synchronization speeds, reduced email client responsiveness, or degraded overall performance. Periodically archiving older messages, reducing mailbox clutter, and optimizing mailbox storage utilization dramatically improves mailbox performance, accelerates synchronization processes, and enhances user email experiences across multiple devices and client platforms. Archiving maintains manageable, efficient mailboxes strategically balanced between active messaging repositories and historical archived content, optimizing mailbox usability, productivity, and performance responsiveness proactively.

Effective email archiving practices within IMAP environments frequently involve comprehensive documentation detailing archiving policies, retention schedules, folder structures, automated methodologies, compliance management procedures, storage optimization strategies, security protections, and archival retrieval mechanisms. Documented archiving practices provide administrators and compliance officers detailed procedural guidance, ensure consistent archival management practices, simplify administrative oversight, and facilitate effective knowledge transfer among relevant personnel. Thorough documentation enhances administrative efficiency, reduces operational complexities, minimizes human errors, and ensures archival practices remain consistently compliant, efficient, and optimized according to organizational archiving objectives.

Continuous monitoring and reporting significantly enhance email archiving efficiency within IMAP infrastructures. Effective monitoring solutions continuously observe archival processes, automated email relocation activities, mailbox storage utilization trends, compliance adherence statuses, search retrieval performance, and archival infrastructure resource allocation. Real-time monitoring dashboards proactively identify potential archiving bottlenecks, incomplete archival operations, storage resource constraints, or compliance deviations, automatically generating administrative alerts facilitating rapid intervention and resolution. Regular archival reporting summarizes archival activities, verifies policy adherence, validates compliance obligations, and informs strategic improvements, storage optimization initiatives, or infrastructure investments continuously enhancing IMAP archival effectiveness.

Continuous innovation and technological advancements ensure IMAP email archiving solutions remain highly responsive, scalable, secure, and adaptive. Emerging innovations introduce advanced archival methodologies, optimized storage management strategies, intelligent automation capabilities, improved search and retrieval functionalities, enhanced security protections, and sophisticated compliance management features. Continuous evolution ensures IMAP email archiving remains effectively capable of addressing contemporary archival complexities, evolving regulatory compliance mandates, growing email management demands, and technological advancements characteristic of modern digital communication environments.

Compliance and Legal Considerations

Compliance and legal considerations are vital elements in the deployment, operation, and management of IMAP-based email systems. As organizations increasingly rely on email as a primary method of communication, email content, metadata, and attachments often become subject to a broad array of regulatory, legal, and corporate governance requirements. Ensuring IMAP infrastructures comply with applicable legal frameworks is essential not only to mitigate risk but also to protect the organization against legal exposure, reputational damage, and financial penalties. Properly addressing compliance mandates requires strategic planning, robust security controls, retention management, and well-documented operational procedures tailored to industry-specific regulations and broader international legal frameworks.

One of the most pressing considerations in IMAP environments is email retention. Regulatory bodies and industry-specific standards frequently require organizations to retain email communications for defined periods, sometimes ranging from several years to indefinitely, depending on the nature of the information and the jurisdiction. Regulations such as the Sarbanes-Oxley Act (SOX), the General Data Protection Regulation (GDPR), and the Health Insurance Portability and Accountability Act (HIPAA) mandate strict retention, handling, and disposal policies for digital communications. IMAP infrastructures must integrate retention policies that automatically enforce these requirements. This typically involves leveraging server-based automation to archive messages based on message age, content, or other criteria and preserving these messages in compliance with legal timeframes. Implementing automated IMAP retention strategies ensures the organization consistently meets regulatory obligations while minimizing human error.

Equally important to retention is the ability to ensure proper data protection and confidentiality within IMAP environments. Many industries mandate strict data protection measures to safeguard personal data, sensitive information, or proprietary business content contained within email messages. IMAP infrastructures must employ robust security protocols such as TLS encryption for message transmission and robust access control mechanisms that restrict email access to authorized personnel only. Encryption ensures that intercepted messages remain unreadable to unauthorized parties, and strict authentication methods help to protect against unauthorized account access. In addition to protecting sensitive information, these measures are often explicitly required under regulations like GDPR, which imposes strict rules regarding the handling and security of personal data within the European Union and for any organization processing data of EU residents.

A critical aspect of compliance within IMAP-based systems involves eDiscovery and legal holds. In the event of legal proceedings or regulatory investigations, organizations may be required to preserve and produce specific email communications as part of formal discovery processes. IMAP infrastructures must support reliable and legally defensible methods to identify, collect, and preserve relevant email data. Organizations frequently implement legal hold procedures within their IMAP environments, preventing specific emails or entire mailboxes from being deleted or altered while a legal matter is ongoing. This process typically includes archiving solutions that support immutable storage options, ensuring that once messages are flagged for legal holds, they cannot be tampered with or purged. A defensible eDiscovery process is critical in demonstrating compliance with court orders and avoiding sanctions for spoliation or destruction of evidence.

Chain of custody is another essential consideration in IMAP compliance. When emails are preserved for legal or regulatory purposes, maintaining a verifiable record of how the data has been handled is critical. Administrators must implement auditing mechanisms within IMAP environments that log access attempts, modifications, transfers, and deletions of emails and metadata. A transparent, unbroken chain of custody establishes a secure, documented history of how each email has been managed, supporting its admissibility as evidence in legal proceedings. IMAP systems integrated with centralized logging and audit trail functionalities make it possible for organizations to verify and demonstrate compliance with chain-of-custody requirements confidently.

Data residency and cross-border data transfer regulations present additional challenges in IMAP compliance, particularly for multinational organizations. Some jurisdictions impose restrictions on where data, including email content, may be stored or transferred. For example, GDPR imposes specific restrictions on transferring personal data outside of the European Economic Area to countries lacking adequate data protection frameworks. Organizations utilizing IMAP services, especially cloud-based email solutions, must carefully assess and comply with data residency laws by ensuring that email data is stored within permitted jurisdictions or implementing contractual safeguards, such as Standard Contractual Clauses (SCCs) or Binding Corporate Rules (BCRs), where applicable. Proper management of data residency and cross-border data transfers is critical to maintaining compliance and avoiding regulatory sanctions.

In addition to these regulatory obligations, organizations must address internal governance and corporate policy requirements related to email usage, content management, and user accountability. Many organizations enforce acceptable use policies governing employee conduct within email systems, restricting the types of content transmitted and ensuring that employees adhere to ethical and professional communication standards. IMAP infrastructures can support these policies by integrating with data loss prevention (DLP) tools, email content filtering systems, and monitoring solutions capable of detecting and blocking policy violations. DLP solutions help prevent unauthorized transmission of sensitive data, while content filters enforce organizational policies on prohibited or inappropriate content within email communications.

Incident response readiness is another key component of compliance within IMAP environments. Organizations must establish formal incident response plans detailing how email-related data breaches, unauthorized access attempts, or compliance violations will be handled. An effective incident response plan should outline immediate containment actions, investigation procedures, notification protocols, and remediation steps to mitigate damage and comply with mandatory breach notification laws. For instance, GDPR mandates notification to supervisory authorities and affected individuals within a short timeframe following certain types of data breaches. IMAP systems integrated with real-time threat detection and alerting mechanisms are essential in identifying potential breaches early and triggering incident response workflows in a timely and compliant manner.

Employee training and awareness initiatives are essential complements to technical compliance controls within IMAP environments. Ensuring that staff members understand regulatory requirements, organizational policies, and the proper use of email systems significantly reduces the likelihood of compliance breaches caused by human error. Regular compliance training sessions covering topics such as phishing awareness, data protection principles, legal hold procedures, and appropriate email usage foster a culture of compliance and accountability, reinforcing the effectiveness of IMAP security and governance measures.

Organizations must also regularly audit their IMAP infrastructure to assess compliance posture and identify areas for improvement. Compliance audits typically involve reviewing retention configurations, testing eDiscovery processes, evaluating security controls, analyzing audit logs, and verifying that all policies align with current legal frameworks and industry best practices. Periodic audits and internal reviews ensure that the IMAP environment continues to meet regulatory expectations, remains secure, and adapts to evolving legal and technological landscapes.

By addressing retention, security, legal hold, chain of custody, data residency, governance policies, incident response, and staff education, organizations create a comprehensive compliance framework for IMAP environments. A proactive, well-rounded approach to compliance and legal considerations ensures that IMAP infrastructures not only meet external regulatory requirements but also promote operational resilience, data integrity, and user accountability within modern digital communication ecosystems.

Security Risks in IMAP Implementations

IMAP, as one of the most widely used protocols for accessing and managing email on remote servers, provides convenience and flexibility, but also introduces a variety of security risks that administrators and organizations must carefully address. IMAP implementations that lack proper security controls or are improperly configured can expose organizations to numerous vulnerabilities, including unauthorized access, data breaches, interception of sensitive communications, and exploitation by malicious actors. Understanding and mitigating these risks is essential for protecting user privacy, safeguarding corporate data, and maintaining the integrity of email communications.

One of the most common security risks associated with IMAP is the transmission of unencrypted data between clients and servers. IMAP was originally designed to operate over plaintext connections, meaning that without modern security enhancements, all data—including user credentials, email content, and metadata—could be exposed to eavesdropping or interception by attackers capable of monitoring network traffic. Such man-in-the-middle attacks can easily capture usernames and passwords if IMAP sessions are not secured using Transport Layer Security (TLS) or its predecessor, Secure Sockets Layer (SSL). Failing to enforce encryption leaves communications vulnerable, particularly on unsecured networks such as public Wi-Fi, where attackers often scan for open, unprotected traffic streams.

Credential theft represents another significant risk in IMAP implementations. Since IMAP relies heavily on password-based authentication, compromised or weak passwords expose user accounts to unauthorized access. Attackers frequently employ brute-force attacks or dictionary attacks against IMAP servers, attempting to guess user credentials through automated tools. Inadequate password policies, such as the absence of complexity requirements or password expiration, exacerbate this risk. Additionally, many IMAP implementations are vulnerable to credential stuffing attacks, where attackers leverage previously breached username-password pairs from other services to attempt unauthorized logins on IMAP accounts.

Misconfigurations within IMAP servers also contribute to security vulnerabilities. Improperly configured permissions, open ports exposed to the internet, and default settings left unchanged can create exploitable entry points for attackers. Some IMAP servers, for instance, may be configured to permit cleartext authentication or may allow anonymous access to certain mailboxes. Others might expose administrative interfaces or APIs without sufficient authentication or network restrictions. Attackers who discover misconfigured IMAP servers can exploit these weaknesses to gain unauthorized access, extract sensitive emails, or pivot deeper into the internal network.

Another risk lies in the handling of user session information. IMAP sessions are typically persistent, and poorly managed session states may expose email accounts to session hijacking. Attackers able to intercept or steal session tokens may impersonate legitimate users without needing to know the account password, bypassing authentication controls. This risk is heightened in shared computing environments or scenarios where users fail to terminate sessions properly, leaving valid sessions open and exploitable.

Phishing campaigns and social engineering attacks also exploit IMAP vulnerabilities indirectly. Since IMAP synchronizes emails across devices, a compromised IMAP account can serve as a distribution point for internal phishing emails that appear to originate from trusted sources. Attackers who gain access to a legitimate IMAP account may leverage it to send convincing phishing emails to other users within the same organization, increasing the likelihood of further account compromises or malicious payload delivery. Such lateral movement can escalate the severity of an attack from a single compromised account to a widespread network security incident.

Inadequate logging and monitoring capabilities within IMAP environments present additional risks by delaying detection and response to security incidents. Many IMAP servers lack detailed logging by default or fail to log critical security events, such as failed login attempts, suspicious session activities, or unusual mailbox access patterns. Without centralized logging and proactive monitoring in place, administrators may be unaware of ongoing brute-force attempts, account compromises, or unauthorized data exfiltration, allowing attackers to persist undetected within the system for extended periods.

Vulnerabilities within IMAP server software itself also contribute to security risks. Like all software, IMAP servers may contain flaws such as buffer overflows, input validation errors, or privilege escalation vulnerabilities. Attackers who exploit these weaknesses can execute arbitrary code, gain elevated privileges, or disrupt server operations through denial-of-service (DoS) attacks. Regularly applying security patches and updates is essential to mitigating this risk, as outdated IMAP software often contains publicly known vulnerabilities that can be exploited by even low-sophistication attackers.

Mail storage exposure is another critical risk, particularly when IMAP servers store email messages in plaintext within back-end file systems or databases without adequate encryption at rest. If an attacker gains unauthorized access to the storage layer—either through direct server compromise or insider threats—they may extract entire mailboxes, including confidential or proprietary information. Organizations failing to implement encryption at rest for stored emails risk exposing sensitive business communications, financial data, personal information, and intellectual property.

Email attachments also present risks in IMAP implementations. Attachments may contain malicious payloads, including ransomware, remote access trojans (RATs), or exploits targeting client-side vulnerabilities. Since IMAP servers often support automatic synchronization and download of attachments across devices, a single malicious file introduced into one account can propagate across all devices linked to that mailbox. Users opening these attachments on vulnerable devices may inadvertently execute malicious code, leading to endpoint compromise or broader organizational breaches.

To mitigate these security risks, organizations must enforce a comprehensive set of security controls within IMAP implementations. This includes mandating the use of TLS for all IMAP connections, implementing strong password policies combined with multi-factor authentication (MFA), regularly auditing server configurations, and limiting IMAP access to trusted IP addresses where possible. Centralized logging solutions, security information and event management (SIEM) systems, and intrusion detection/prevention systems (IDS/IPS) should be deployed to monitor IMAP-related activity and alert administrators to anomalies in real time.

Security awareness training also plays a critical role in addressing risks, as users must recognize phishing attempts, manage sessions responsibly, and adhere to corporate security policies. In parallel, organizations must continuously update IMAP server software, patch security vulnerabilities promptly, and employ endpoint protection to defend against malicious attachments and client-side exploits.

Ultimately, while IMAP offers powerful and flexible email access, it also introduces a diverse set of security risks that can be exploited if appropriate defenses are not established. By recognizing the inherent vulnerabilities in IMAP implementations and applying a layered security strategy, organizations can significantly reduce the likelihood of breaches, data loss, and service disruptions while ensuring that email services remain secure and resilient in an increasingly hostile threat landscape.

Modern Authentication Protocols (OAuth2) with IMAP

The evolution of authentication mechanisms within IMAP environments has brought significant improvements in both security and user experience, particularly with the adoption of modern authentication protocols such as OAuth2. Traditional IMAP authentication methods typically rely on username and password combinations, transmitted during the login phase to validate user identity. However, as cyber threats have become more sophisticated and widespread, relying solely on static credentials has proven insufficient to safeguard email communications. OAuth2, as a modern, token-based authentication framework, offers enhanced protection by eliminating the need for users to transmit their actual passwords during the authentication process, reducing the risk of credential theft, phishing, and other common security threats.

OAuth2 operates as an authorization framework that grants applications limited access to user resources without exposing user credentials. When integrated with IMAP, OAuth2 allows email clients to access users' mailboxes by using time-limited access tokens, which are issued by an identity provider (IdP) or authorization server. The OAuth2 process typically involves several stages, beginning with the user granting consent for a client application, such as an email client, to access their mailbox. The authorization server, after authenticating the user using secure methods such as multi-factor authentication, issues an access token to the client, enabling it to connect to the IMAP server on behalf of the user.

This shift to token-based authentication significantly reduces the attack surface of IMAP implementations. Access tokens are ephemeral by design, usually valid only for a short period, limiting their usefulness to attackers even if tokens are intercepted. Additionally, tokens can be configured with granular scopes, specifying exactly what resources the client can access and what actions it can perform. For example, a token may grant read-only access to a user's inbox without permitting the client to send emails or modify mailbox settings. This fine-grained control over permissions enhances overall security posture and aligns with the principle of least privilege, which dictates that applications should operate with the minimal level of access required to complete their functions.

OAuth2 with IMAP also introduces improvements in session management and revocation capabilities. Unlike traditional password-based authentication, where revoking a session often requires a password reset or account lockout, OAuth2 tokens can be revoked individually by the identity provider without disrupting other sessions or applications linked to the same user account. This allows administrators to respond to security incidents more efficiently, immediately invalidating potentially compromised tokens while allowing legitimate sessions to continue unaffected. OAuth2 also facilitates the use of refresh tokens, enabling client applications to request new access tokens seamlessly without requiring users to re-authenticate frequently. This enhances user experience while maintaining secure, uninterrupted access to IMAP mailboxes.

The adoption of OAuth2 across major identity providers, including Microsoft Azure Active Directory, Google Identity Platform, and Okta, has standardized secure authentication practices within IMAP implementations. These identity providers support OAuth2 flows such as the Authorization Code Grant, which is commonly used for web-based applications and supports enhanced security features like Proof Key for Code Exchange (PKCE). PKCE helps mitigate authorization code interception attacks by binding the code exchange to a specific client session, further securing the authentication process in public or mobile environments. IMAP clients integrated with OAuth2 leverage these industry-standard flows, ensuring secure authentication in both web-based and desktop email applications.

Integrating OAuth2 into IMAP environments also helps organizations comply with modern security and privacy regulations, including GDPR, HIPAA, and CCPA, by reducing the exposure of sensitive user credentials. OAuth2 minimizes the risk associated with credential reuse, a common vector exploited in credential stuffing attacks, where attackers leverage stolen username-password pairs from previous breaches to compromise additional accounts. Since OAuth2 does not require clients to store or transmit user passwords, it reduces the likelihood of such attacks succeeding within IMAP-based email systems.

From a deployment perspective, configuring IMAP to support OAuth2 typically involves modifications on both the IMAP server and the client application. The IMAP server must be capable of validating OAuth2 tokens received from the client, which requires integration with the organization's chosen identity provider. This may involve enabling token introspection endpoints, configuring JSON Web Token (JWT) verification, or supporting OpenID Connect (OIDC) protocols, which extend OAuth2 to include user identity information. Client applications must also be updated to support OAuth2 authorization flows, including handling redirects to authorization servers, managing token storage securely, and including the access token in the IMAP LOGIN or AUTHENTICATE commands.

Additionally, the transition to OAuth2 in IMAP environments enhances visibility and control for administrators. Identity providers that support OAuth2 typically provide detailed logging, reporting, and analytics on authentication events, including information about which applications accessed user mailboxes, when access occurred, and from which geographic locations. This increased visibility improves the organization's ability to detect suspicious activity, enforce compliance policies, and conduct forensic investigations following security incidents.

The widespread adoption of OAuth2 has led to the deprecation of older, less secure protocols such as Basic Authentication in many enterprise environments. Major service providers like Microsoft have publicly announced the retirement of Basic Authentication for IMAP access to cloud services like Exchange Online, encouraging customers to migrate to OAuth2-based modern authentication solutions. This industry trend reflects a broader shift toward zero-trust security models, where continuous verification of identity, secure access controls, and granular session management are prioritized over legacy credential-based systems.

OAuth2 also supports seamless integration with other security-enhancing technologies such as single sign-on (SSO) and conditional access policies. SSO reduces password fatigue by allowing users to access multiple services, including their IMAP email accounts, using a single set of credentials. Conditional access policies enable organizations to enforce additional security requirements based on contextual factors, such as device compliance, user risk level, or geographic location. For example, an organization might configure its identity provider to block IMAP access via OAuth2 from untrusted networks or require additional multi-factor authentication steps when abnormal login behavior is detected.

Despite its numerous advantages, organizations implementing OAuth2 with IMAP must still address potential risks, such as improper token storage on client devices or vulnerabilities within third-party applications that use OAuth2 tokens to access IMAP accounts. It is critical that OAuth2 tokens are securely encrypted at rest and that client-side implementations adhere to best practices for token handling, such as limiting token scope, enforcing secure HTTPS communications, and promptly revoking tokens when no longer needed.

In summary, the integration of modern authentication protocols like OAuth2 within IMAP environments represents a significant step forward in securing email communications. By replacing traditional password-based authentication with token-driven access control, OAuth2 dramatically reduces the risks of credential theft, unauthorized access, and session hijacking. It also improves administrative control, supports regulatory compliance, and enhances the user experience. As organizations continue to adopt OAuth2, they move closer to implementing comprehensive, secure, and scalable authentication frameworks capable of meeting the demands of the modern digital landscape.

IMAP and Email Encryption

IMAP and email encryption are closely intertwined in the broader context of securing electronic communications. IMAP, or Internet Message Access Protocol, provides users with remote access to email stored on a server, enabling them to retrieve, manage, and synchronize email messages across multiple devices. However, while IMAP excels in offering flexible and centralized access to mailboxes, it does not natively provide content-level protection for the emails it handles. For this reason, combining IMAP with robust encryption mechanisms is essential to protect the confidentiality, integrity, and authenticity of email messages in transit and at rest.

A key component of securing IMAP communications is the use of transport layer encryption. The most common method for securing IMAP connections is by implementing Transport Layer Security (TLS), which encrypts the communication channel between the IMAP client and the server. Without TLS, IMAP traffic, including usernames, passwords, and message contents, can be intercepted and read by attackers monitoring the network. TLS creates a secure tunnel that prevents eavesdropping and man-in-the-middle attacks. There are two primary ways to use TLS with IMAP: implicit TLS, where the client connects to the server on port 993 and starts with encryption immediately, and explicit TLS, where the client connects to the server on port 143 and upgrades the connection to TLS using the STARTTLS command. Both methods are widely supported and critical for maintaining secure communication channels.

While TLS protects messages in transit, it does not encrypt the email content itself. Once emails reach the server or the client, they are decrypted and remain accessible to anyone with access to the system. This limitation highlights the need for end-to-end encryption (E2EE) to safeguard the actual content of email messages. Two prominent standards for email encryption at the message level are Pretty Good Privacy (PGP) and Secure/Multipurpose Internet Mail Extensions (S/MIME). These encryption protocols ensure that only the intended recipient, possessing the corresponding private key, can decrypt and read the email's contents, regardless of the security of the transmission channel or the mail server.

PGP and S/MIME both rely on public key infrastructure (PKI) to exchange encrypted messages. In a typical PGP workflow, the sender encrypts the email using the recipient's public key. The recipient then decrypts the message using their private key. This guarantees that only the intended recipient can access the message content. S/MIME functions similarly but is often integrated directly into corporate environments through the use of digital certificates issued by trusted certificate authorities (CAs). S/MIME not only provides encryption but also supports digital signing, which allows the sender to prove their identity and ensures message integrity by preventing tampering.

IMAP works seamlessly with both PGP and S/MIME, as the protocol simply handles the transport and synchronization of email messages between the server and client. Since the encryption and decryption processes occur at the application layer within the email client, IMAP remains agnostic to whether the message content is encrypted. This modular design allows organizations to implement encryption standards based on their specific security requirements while still leveraging IMAP's powerful mailbox management capabilities.

Another important consideration is encryption at rest. When emails are stored on an IMAP server, they must be protected against unauthorized access, especially in environments where server breaches or insider threats are possible. Many organizations implement full disk encryption (FDE) or encrypt specific email storage volumes to prevent email data from being readable if the underlying hardware is stolen or compromised. More advanced configurations also include database-level encryption or file-level encryption for email storage repositories. Encryption at rest, combined with robust access controls and audit logging, ensures that emails remain secure even when stored on IMAP servers for extended periods.

Modern IMAP servers often support integration with secure key management systems (KMS) to handle the storage and management of encryption keys. A centralized KMS allows administrators to enforce policies around key rotation, expiration, and access control, further enhancing the security posture of IMAP infrastructures. Integrating encryption mechanisms with KMS solutions ensures that key management is handled securely, minimizing risks associated with improper key storage or unauthorized access to encryption keys.

Beyond protecting email content, encryption also plays a role in securing IMAP authentication mechanisms. Modern authentication protocols, such as OAuth2, often operate over TLS-secured connections and may encrypt tokens used to access IMAP services. Additionally, organizations deploying multifactor authentication (MFA) further reduce the risk of account compromise by requiring users to present additional verification factors, such as hardware tokens or biometric data, in addition to encrypted credentials.

Despite its importance, encryption introduces challenges in IMAP environments, particularly concerning search functionality and server-side filtering. Since end-to-end encrypted emails are encrypted before they are transmitted via IMAP and decrypted only on the recipient's client device, the IMAP server cannot index or search the contents of encrypted emails. This limitation requires organizations to balance security requirements with usability considerations, especially in environments where server-side search and filtering capabilities are critical. Some organizations address this by implementing client-side search tools or selectively encrypting sensitive communications while leaving less critical emails in plaintext.

Moreover, encrypted email environments require thorough user training and awareness programs to ensure users understand how to handle encryption keys, recognize signed emails, and identify when encryption is or is not in use. Mismanagement of encryption tools can lead to situations where sensitive emails are sent unencrypted, private keys are lost, or encrypted emails become inaccessible due to key mismatches. Ensuring that encryption best practices are consistently followed by all users helps prevent security lapses and maintains the integrity of the encrypted communication ecosystem.

Compliance is another major driver for implementing encryption in IMAP environments. Regulations such as the General Data Protection Regulation (GDPR), the Health Insurance Portability and Accountability Act (HIPAA), and the Payment Card Industry Data Security Standard (PCI DSS) require organizations to protect sensitive information, including emails, with appropriate security measures. Failure to secure emails properly can result in regulatory fines, legal action, and reputational damage. Implementing encryption for IMAP traffic and email content helps organizations meet compliance obligations and demonstrate their commitment to protecting sensitive communications.

Combining IMAP with robust encryption practices forms the foundation for secure email communication in today's threat landscape. While IMAP provides reliable, centralized mailbox access, encryption technologies protect the actual content of those communications, both in transit and at rest. By leveraging transport encryption, message-level encryption, and storage encryption, organizations can significantly enhance their email security posture, reduce their exposure to cyber threats, and comply with regulatory mandates, all while continuing to enjoy the flexibility and functionality that IMAP provides.

Containerization of IMAP Services

Containerization has emerged as a transformative approach in modern IT infrastructure, and its application to IMAP services offers significant benefits in terms of deployment flexibility, scalability, portability, and resource efficiency. IMAP, as a widely used protocol for accessing and managing email stored on a server, is traditionally deployed on dedicated physical servers or virtual machines. However, containerization introduces a paradigm shift by packaging IMAP services into lightweight, portable containers that can run consistently across various environments. Leveraging container technology such as Docker allows organizations to streamline the deployment and management of IMAP servers, while enhancing security, reliability, and operational agility.

At the core of containerization is the concept of encapsulating the IMAP server application, its dependencies, configurations, and runtime environment into an isolated container image. This image can then be instantiated as a running container, guaranteeing consistent behavior regardless of the underlying infrastructure, whether it is an on-premises data center, a cloud platform, or a hybrid environment. By eliminating dependency conflicts and environmental inconsistencies, containerization simplifies the IMAP service deployment process and enables faster, more reliable rollouts of new instances or updates.

One of the most significant advantages of containerizing IMAP services is the improved scalability it offers. Containers are lightweight compared to traditional virtual machines, allowing organizations to deploy multiple IMAP server instances on a single physical host or across a cluster with minimal overhead. This enables horizontal scaling, where additional containers can be launched on demand to handle spikes in user activity, large volumes of incoming connections, or increased email traffic. Container orchestration platforms such as Kubernetes or Docker Swarm can be employed to automate the scaling process, dynamically adjusting the number of running IMAP containers based on resource utilization metrics or predefined policies. This elasticity ensures optimal resource allocation and high availability, even during peak usage periods.

Containerization also facilitates the microservices architecture approach, where the IMAP service can be decoupled from other email-related services such as SMTP for outbound mail, antivirus scanning, antispam filtering, or directory services like LDAP. Each service can be deployed as an independent container, communicating through defined interfaces such as APIs or message queues. This modular design enhances fault isolation, improves maintainability, and allows individual services to be updated, scaled, or replaced without impacting the entire email system. For example, administrators can update the IMAP container with security patches or new features while leaving other services unaffected, reducing system downtime and minimizing operational risks.

From a development and testing perspective, containerization significantly accelerates the software lifecycle for IMAP services. Developers and administrators can build container images containing the exact version of the IMAP server software and its dependencies used in production. These images can be tested in staging or development environments that faithfully replicate production conditions, ensuring consistent behavior and reducing the likelihood of environment-related issues when transitioning to live systems. Continuous integration and continuous deployment (CI/CD) pipelines can be easily integrated with container workflows, enabling rapid development cycles and automated deployments of IMAP containers across multiple environments.

Security benefits also arise from containerizing IMAP services. Containers provide process-level isolation through the use of kernel namespaces and control groups (cgroups), limiting the impact of potential security breaches. If an attacker compromises one container, they are typically confined to that isolated environment and cannot easily affect other containers or the host system. In addition, container images can be hardened by removing unnecessary packages, libraries, and components, reducing the attack surface. Security scanning tools can analyze container images for known vulnerabilities, ensuring that only secure and compliant images are promoted to production. Runtime security solutions further enhance protection by monitoring container behavior, detecting anomalous activities, and enforcing security policies.

Portability is another compelling advantage of IMAP containerization. Containerized IMAP services can be deployed across a wide range of platforms, including bare-metal servers, virtual machines, private clouds, public clouds, or hybrid environments, without requiring modifications. This portability enables organizations to adopt multi-cloud strategies, avoiding vendor lock-in and enabling disaster recovery capabilities through the rapid redeployment of IMAP containers to alternative environments in the event of outages or disasters. The ability to replicate entire IMAP server environments quickly and reliably supports business continuity and operational resilience.

Monitoring and management of containerized IMAP services are enhanced by integration with container orchestration platforms and observability tools. Kubernetes, for instance, provides built-in capabilities for service discovery, load balancing, health checks, and self-healing through automatic container restarts or replacements. Combined with monitoring tools such as Prometheus and Grafana, administrators gain real-time visibility into resource consumption, application performance, and infrastructure health. Logging solutions such as Fluentd or the ELK stack (Elasticsearch, Logstash, Kibana) can aggregate and analyze logs generated by IMAP containers, supporting effective troubleshooting and operational insights.

Despite its numerous advantages, containerizing IMAP services also presents challenges that organizations must address. Persistent storage is a key consideration, as IMAP servers require reliable and performant storage for mailboxes and message data. Containers are inherently ephemeral, meaning that data stored within a container is lost if the container is terminated or rescheduled. To overcome this limitation, administrators can leverage persistent storage volumes provided by container orchestration platforms or external storage systems. Network-attached storage (NAS), storage area networks (SAN), or cloud-based storage solutions can be integrated to ensure data persistence across container lifecycles.

Another challenge relates to performance tuning and resource allocation. Since multiple containers may share the same underlying host, it is essential to configure resource limits and requests properly to prevent resource contention or starvation. Administrators must carefully allocate CPU, memory, and I/O resources to IMAP containers based on workload demands, ensuring consistent performance and stability. Benchmarking and load testing are recommended practices to determine optimal resource configurations for containerized IMAP deployments.

Containerization of IMAP services marks a significant advancement in how modern email infrastructures are designed and managed. By enabling lightweight, scalable, and portable deployments, containerization enhances operational efficiency, security, and flexibility. Organizations adopting containerized IMAP solutions gain the ability to respond quickly to changing business needs, deploy services across diverse environments, and maintain high availability and performance. As container ecosystems continue to mature, the benefits of deploying IMAP services within containers will only become more pronounced, offering a future-proof approach to modern email service management.

IMAP Integration with Collaboration Tools

The integration of IMAP with modern collaboration tools has become a key driver in enhancing productivity, streamlining communication workflows, and providing seamless user experiences across distributed teams. While IMAP is fundamentally designed as a protocol for accessing and managing emails on a remote server, its role within modern business ecosystems has expanded as organizations increasingly adopt collaboration platforms such as calendars, task managers, messaging apps, and document-sharing tools. By connecting IMAP-enabled email services with collaborative software, users benefit from consolidated access to communication channels, improved data synchronization, and the ability to manage projects and tasks directly from their email environment.

A common use case of IMAP integration is the synchronization of email with calendar and scheduling applications. Many collaboration tools, such as Microsoft Outlook, Google Workspace, and Zoho Mail, provide native integration of IMAP email accounts with calendar functionalities. This integration allows users to convert incoming emails into calendar events or meeting invitations directly from their inboxes. For instance, when an IMAP user receives an email containing project deadlines or meeting requests, integrated calendar tools can automatically extract dates, times, and relevant information to create event entries. This seamless workflow eliminates the need to manually transfer information between applications, reducing human error and improving scheduling efficiency.

Task management is another area where IMAP integration with collaboration tools proves valuable. By linking IMAP email accounts to project management platforms such as Trello, Asana, or Monday.com, users can generate tasks or action items from specific emails. Many task management systems offer plugins or automation features that allow users to forward emails to designated boards or lists, creating tasks with the content of the email as context. This integration ensures that important messages are not overlooked and are instead converted into actionable tasks that can be prioritized, assigned, and tracked within the project management workflow. Furthermore, some advanced solutions automatically parse task-related information from emails, including due dates, assigned personnel, and attached documents, facilitating efficient task creation without leaving the email client.

Real-time messaging platforms, such as Slack or Microsoft Teams, also benefit from IMAP integration, enabling users to bridge asynchronous email communication with instant messaging workflows. Through integrations with IMAP, these messaging platforms can monitor designated inbox folders or labels, triggering notifications when new emails arrive. For example, critical customer inquiries received via email can be automatically forwarded or posted to a specific Slack channel where support teams can collaborate in real time to address the issue. Such integrations create unified communication streams, bringing the speed and convenience of instant messaging to the traditionally asynchronous world of email.

Document management systems further enhance collaboration when integrated with IMAP services. Tools such as Google Drive, SharePoint, or Dropbox allow users to directly link email attachments from IMAP-connected accounts to centralized file repositories. Instead of downloading attachments locally, users can save documents from incoming emails to shared folders accessible by the entire team. Some systems also offer automatic attachment extraction and storage, organizing files based on email metadata such as sender, subject, or project identifiers. This integration streamlines document sharing and version control processes, ensuring that critical files remain accessible, organized, and properly tracked across collaborative environments.

The automation of workflows through integration with IMAP is another growing trend, particularly through platforms such as Zapier, Make (formerly Integromat), or Microsoft Power Automate. These automation platforms connect IMAP email services with hundreds of third-party applications, allowing users to build customized workflows triggered by email activity. For example, when a specific type of email is received, an automation can extract relevant information and update a CRM record, create a new helpdesk ticket, or send an acknowledgment email to the sender. Automating routine tasks not only saves time but also ensures that business processes remain consistent and error-free.

Collaboration tools integrated with IMAP services also enable unified search capabilities across communication channels. Users can leverage advanced search engines that aggregate data from email inboxes, chat logs, task boards, and document repositories, providing a holistic view of project-related information. These integrated search features allow users to find relevant emails, messages, documents, and tasks without switching between multiple platforms, fostering more efficient knowledge management and reducing time spent locating critical information.

Security and compliance considerations are essential when integrating IMAP with collaboration tools. Organizations must ensure that data transferred between IMAP services and third-party applications is encrypted both in transit and at rest. OAuth2 has become the de facto standard for securing IMAP integrations, allowing users to authorize external applications to access their email data without sharing passwords. Proper implementation of OAuth2 ensures that permissions granted to collaboration tools are limited in scope and duration, reducing the risk of unauthorized access. Additionally, administrators must implement monitoring solutions and audit trails to track integration activity, ensuring that sensitive email content remains compliant with internal policies and regulatory requirements.

The integration of IMAP with mobile collaboration apps is particularly valuable for remote workers and distributed teams. Many mobile productivity suites offer seamless access to IMAP inboxes alongside project management tools, calendars, and messaging apps. This mobile-first approach enables users to respond to emails, update project tasks, schedule meetings, and collaborate with colleagues from anywhere, enhancing agility and responsiveness. Push notifications from integrated apps ensure that users are immediately informed of new emails or project updates, promoting timely decision-making and continuous engagement with collaborative workflows.

Integrating IMAP services with customer relationship management (CRM) platforms further streamlines business operations by linking email correspondence with client records. For example, CRM solutions such as Salesforce, HubSpot, or Zoho CRM can automatically log email interactions from IMAP-connected accounts, enriching customer profiles with complete communication histories. This enables sales and support teams to access contextual information about customer interactions directly within the CRM, improving customer service quality, follow-up accuracy, and sales pipeline visibility.

Incorporating IMAP services into collaborative ecosystems transforms email from a stand-alone communication channel into a deeply integrated component of organizational workflows. By bridging IMAP email access with task management, real-time messaging, document sharing, automation platforms, and CRM tools, organizations empower teams to collaborate more effectively, streamline processes, and improve overall productivity. This integrated approach ensures that critical information from email communication is efficiently harnessed across multiple platforms, supporting informed decision-making and fostering a cohesive, collaborative digital workspace.

IMAP API Development

IMAP API development plays a crucial role in enabling applications to interact programmatically with email servers, facilitating the automation of email-related tasks, enhancing application functionality, and streamlining communication workflows. IMAP, as a protocol, provides a standardized set of commands for managing email messages stored on a remote server, including capabilities for reading, moving, deleting, and organizing emails within folders. Developing APIs that leverage IMAP involves building interfaces or libraries that abstract the underlying IMAP commands, making it easier for developers to integrate email functionality into their applications without dealing directly with low-level protocol details.

One of the key components of IMAP API development is the creation of robust connection management mechanisms. IMAP operates over TCP connections and requires the client to maintain an active session with the server during operations such as fetching emails or modifying folder structures. A well-designed IMAP API must handle connection establishment, session persistence, timeout management, and graceful termination of connections to avoid resource leaks and improve reliability. Additionally, APIs must be able to recover from network interruptions by re-establishing dropped connections or re-authenticating sessions when necessary, ensuring seamless operation in unstable network environments.

Authentication handling is another critical aspect of IMAP API development. Modern IMAP APIs need to support a range of authentication methods, from traditional username and password combinations to more secure mechanisms such as OAuth2. Implementing OAuth2 requires the API to handle token acquisition, token refresh workflows, and the secure storage of access and refresh tokens. APIs must also be designed to integrate with various identity providers, allowing applications to authenticate IMAP sessions in compliance with modern security and regulatory requirements.

A fundamental part of the IMAP API is its capability to abstract and simplify the issuance of IMAP commands such as SELECT, FETCH, STORE, SEARCH, APPEND, and EXPUNGE. These commands form the basis of nearly all IMAP operations, and the API must provide user-friendly methods or functions that translate higher-level operations into the appropriate IMAP command sequences. For example, an API method designed to retrieve the most recent unread emails might internally issue a SEARCH command for unseen messages followed by a FETCH command to download message headers and bodies. Such abstractions save developers time and reduce the complexity of implementing email features in their applications.

Another important feature in IMAP API development is support for mailbox and folder management. APIs should offer comprehensive methods to create, delete, rename, and list folders within user mailboxes. These methods must handle the hierarchical nature of IMAP folders, taking into account namespace conventions and delimiter characters that vary between IMAP server implementations. Properly managing folder hierarchies within the API ensures that applications can organize emails effectively, supporting user workflows such as project-based email categorization or automated message routing.

Message parsing and handling is also a core responsibility of any IMAP API. Email messages are often multipart documents containing plain text, HTML content, and a variety of attachments encoded in different MIME types. The API must be capable of parsing MIME structures, decoding message bodies, and extracting attachments while preserving metadata such as content types, filenames, and encoding information. This functionality is essential for applications that need to process incoming emails, display formatted message content, or manage file attachments as part of automated workflows.

In addition to message parsing, IMAP APIs frequently include support for handling message flags and attributes. IMAP defines several standard flags such as \Seen, \Answered, \Flagged, \Deleted, and \Draft, which indicate message states. The API must provide mechanisms for setting, clearing, and retrieving these flags programmatically, enabling applications to automate tasks such as marking messages as read after processing or flagging important emails for follow-up actions. Support for custom flags and labels is also valuable for applications that require specialized tagging or categorization beyond the standard IMAP flag set.

Search functionality within an IMAP API is another essential feature. The IMAP SEARCH command allows clients to query messages based on various criteria such as date ranges, sender or recipient addresses, subject lines, keywords, and message flags. A well-designed API should offer flexible and intuitive search methods, abstracting the complexity of constructing IMAP search queries. Additionally, APIs should support both basic and advanced search options, allowing developers to build highly targeted queries that improve application efficiency when dealing with large mailboxes or specific message retrieval needs.

IMAP API development also requires careful attention to performance optimization. Since IMAP servers can contain vast numbers of messages and folders, inefficient API implementations may result in unnecessary network traffic or slow response times. Techniques such as selective synchronization, partial message fetching, and server-side filtering help reduce the amount of data transmitted and improve application responsiveness. The API should also provide asynchronous or non-blocking operation modes, allowing applications to perform other tasks while waiting for server responses, which is especially important in web or mobile applications with strict performance requirements.

Error handling and exception management are critical components of any IMAP API. IMAP servers can return a variety of status responses indicating success, failure, or server-side issues such as mailbox lock conflicts, permission errors, or quota limitations. The API must expose these responses clearly to developers, providing detailed error messages, status codes, and recommended remediation actions. By implementing robust error handling, the API helps applications respond gracefully to operational issues, improving reliability and user satisfaction.

Finally, IMAP APIs must address security considerations beyond authentication. This includes implementing protections against common vulnerabilities such as IMAP injection, where specially crafted inputs could manipulate command sequences. Input validation, command sanitization, and strict adherence to IMAP protocol specifications are necessary to mitigate these risks. Additionally, APIs should enforce secure defaults, such as requiring encrypted IMAP connections via TLS and limiting exposure of sensitive logging information.

IMAP API development ultimately empowers developers to build email-aware applications that integrate seamlessly with existing IMAP infrastructures. Whether used for building custom email clients, automating business processes, integrating with CRM systems, or developing productivity tools, a well-constructed IMAP API acts as a bridge between applications and the email ecosystem. By abstracting protocol complexity, offering robust functionality, and addressing critical security and performance concerns, IMAP APIs play a pivotal role in modernizing and extending the capabilities of email systems within diverse technology environments.

Automating IMAP Operations

Automating IMAP operations has become a vital practice for organizations and developers seeking to improve the efficiency, reliability, and scalability of email management processes. As email traffic grows and user expectations demand faster, more consistent handling of messages, manual management of IMAP-based tasks becomes impractical, especially in environments with large mailboxes or high volumes of email. Automation leverages scripts, APIs, and workflow orchestration tools to streamline routine tasks such as message retrieval, categorization, archiving, synchronization, and monitoring. By automating these operations, organizations can significantly reduce administrative overhead, minimize human error, and ensure consistent execution of critical email workflows.

One of the most common IMAP operations to automate is email retrieval. Scripts and applications can be programmed to regularly connect to an IMAP server, authenticate securely using credentials or tokens, and scan inboxes or specified folders for new or unread messages. Automated processes can be configured to filter messages based on a variety of criteria, such as sender addresses, subject keywords, timestamps, or specific message flags. Once matching messages are found, the automation script can download relevant content, including message bodies, headers, and attachments, and route them to the appropriate destination for further processing. For example, customer support systems often automate IMAP retrieval to capture inbound service requests and feed them into ticketing platforms such as Zendesk or ServiceNow.

Archiving and message organization are also ideal candidates for automation within IMAP environments. Scripts can routinely scan mailboxes to identify messages that meet predefined criteria, such as emails older than a specific number of days or messages marked as read. These messages can then be automatically moved to designated archive folders, reducing the size of active inboxes and improving email client performance. Organizations with strict compliance requirements often automate the archiving process to ensure that regulatory policies regarding message retention and storage are consistently enforced across all user accounts. Automation not only accelerates archiving but also eliminates the risk of inconsistencies that arise when relying on manual user actions.

Another common area where IMAP automation is highly valuable is the management of message flags and labels. Automated scripts can apply or remove IMAP flags based on business logic or specific workflows. For instance, messages from VIP clients can be automatically flagged for immediate attention, while system-generated notifications can be labeled and moved to a lower-priority folder for periodic review. Automation ensures that messages are consistently categorized, improving user productivity and enabling more efficient filtering and prioritization within the email client.

Synchronization tasks, particularly in large-scale environments, also benefit from automation. In distributed organizations where employees may rely on multiple devices to access email, ensuring that mailbox states remain consistent across clients is crucial. Automated IMAP synchronization processes can periodically check folder structures, ensure message consistency, and correct discrepancies, such as missing messages or incorrect flag statuses. Automated reconciliation scripts help maintain data integrity across devices, reduce helpdesk tickets related to synchronization issues, and enhance the end-user experience.

Advanced IMAP automation extends to parsing email content and integrating with external systems. Scripts can extract relevant information from message bodies or attachments and trigger downstream workflows. For example, an organization might implement a solution that scans emails for purchase orders, extracts order details, and automatically inserts the data into an enterprise resource planning (ERP) system. This type of automation eliminates manual data entry, reduces processing time, and ensures accuracy when transferring information from emails to other business applications.

Automation is also commonly used to implement email notifications and alerts. Scripts can monitor specific IMAP folders for critical messages and automatically notify designated users via email, SMS, or collaboration platforms such as Slack or Microsoft Teams. This functionality is particularly useful in environments where timely responses are crucial, such as security operations centers or customer service departments. Automated notifications ensure that urgent messages are promptly brought to the attention of the appropriate personnel, improving incident response times and overall operational efficiency.

The integration of IMAP automation with workflow orchestration platforms further enhances its capabilities. Tools such as Zapier, Microsoft Power Automate, or custom-built automation frameworks allow users to create multi-step workflows that combine IMAP actions with other system tasks. For example, a workflow might automatically retrieve emails with invoice attachments, upload them to a document management system, and notify the accounting team via chat application. These low-code and no-code platforms enable non-technical users to build robust IMAP-based workflows, democratizing automation capabilities across different departments within an organization.

Security considerations must be addressed when automating IMAP operations. Scripts and automation platforms should use secure authentication methods, such as OAuth2 tokens, rather than storing plaintext passwords in code or configuration files. TLS encryption should be enforced for all IMAP connections to protect data in transit. Additionally, automated processes should implement error handling and logging mechanisms to detect and respond to unexpected events, such as failed logins, server errors, or invalid message formats. Logs generated by automated IMAP processes provide valuable insights for troubleshooting, auditing, and ensuring compliance with security policies.

Automation of IMAP tasks also supports operational scalability. As organizations grow and email volumes increase, manual processes for managing email become increasingly untenable. Automated workflows can scale horizontally by running on distributed servers, containers, or cloud platforms, processing thousands of messages in parallel without significant additional overhead. Cloud-based automation tools allow IMAP scripts to run in serverless environments, further reducing infrastructure management requirements and enabling cost-effective scaling to meet fluctuating demand.

Finally, the continuous monitoring of IMAP servers through automated scripts helps maintain system health and performance. Automation tools can regularly check server response times, mailbox quotas, folder integrity, and connection stability. Automated health checks can trigger alerts when thresholds are exceeded, such as when a user approaches their mailbox quota or when server latency degrades. By proactively identifying issues, automated monitoring reduces downtime, supports capacity planning, and ensures a consistent user experience across the IMAP infrastructure.

Automating IMAP operations brings significant benefits to organizations by reducing manual workloads, improving process consistency, enhancing security, and enabling seamless integration with broader business systems. Whether applied to simple tasks like email sorting or complex workflows involving multiple external applications, IMAP automation empowers teams to manage email more effectively and focus on higher-value activities that drive business success. As organizations continue to adopt automation as part of their digital transformation strategies, the role of IMAP automation will become increasingly important in supporting modern, agile, and efficient communication ecosystems.

IMAP in Hybrid Email Deployments

IMAP in hybrid email deployments plays a pivotal role in enabling seamless communication between on-premises and cloud-based environments, supporting organizations that choose to operate in a mixed infrastructure model. A hybrid email deployment typically combines on-premises mail servers, such as Microsoft Exchange Server or other IMAP-compatible solutions, with cloud-based platforms like Microsoft 365, Google Workspace, or other IMAP-compliant services. This approach allows businesses to retain control over certain email workloads while leveraging the scalability and accessibility of cloud services. IMAP serves as a critical protocol in these environments by acting as a bridge between disparate email systems and providing consistent access to messages, folders, and mailbox structures across both local and remote infrastructures.

One of the primary reasons organizations adopt hybrid email deployments is to balance flexibility, control, and cost. While cloud-based email platforms offer numerous advantages, such as simplified management and built-in redundancy, some organizations may need to retain on-premises email servers due to regulatory requirements, data sovereignty concerns, or legacy application dependencies. IMAP facilitates the coexistence of these environments by providing a standardized method for accessing email data, enabling users to connect to their mailboxes regardless of where the email is physically stored. This flexibility ensures that employees experience a unified email experience whether their data resides on-premises, in the cloud, or distributed across both.

A key consideration when deploying IMAP in a hybrid environment is the synchronization of mailbox data across the two infrastructures. IMAP inherently supports folder-based synchronization, allowing email clients to maintain consistency in folder hierarchies and message states. For example, when a user moves a message from the inbox to a project-specific folder in their IMAP client, the change is reflected on both the cloud-based and on-premises servers, depending on where the message resides. Hybrid deployments often employ migration tools or middleware that leverage IMAP to facilitate the transfer and synchronization of mailboxes between on-premises servers and cloud platforms. These tools automate the process of copying messages, preserving folder structures, and maintaining message flags such as read/unread or flagged status.

Security and authentication are also central to the successful integration of IMAP in hybrid email environments. Since IMAP traffic typically traverses public networks when connecting to cloud-based email services, it is essential to enforce secure communication protocols such as TLS to protect data in transit. Hybrid deployments must also ensure that authentication mechanisms are unified across both infrastructures. For example, organizations may implement federated identity solutions or directory synchronization tools that allow users to log in using the same credentials for both on-premises and cloud-based mailboxes. OAuth2 is increasingly being adopted in hybrid scenarios to provide secure, token-based authentication for IMAP clients connecting to cloud services while maintaining legacy authentication methods for on-premises servers.

Email routing and message flow are additional factors to consider when using IMAP in a hybrid deployment. Organizations must define clear policies for how incoming and outgoing email traffic is managed between on-premises and cloud infrastructures. In some cases, inbound emails may first arrive at the on-premises server and be forwarded to cloud-based mailboxes, or vice versa. IMAP does not handle mail delivery itself but works in tandem with SMTP for sending messages and with directory services for user management. Routing configurations must ensure that messages are delivered to the correct environment and synchronized appropriately using IMAP to provide users with a consistent view of their email regardless of where the messages originate or are stored.

Another advantage of IMAP in hybrid deployments is its ability to support gradual migration strategies. Organizations that wish to transition from fully on-premises email infrastructures to cloud-based services often opt for a phased migration approach, moving user mailboxes in stages over an extended period. IMAP plays a critical role in this process by allowing users with migrated cloud mailboxes to continue accessing historical emails stored on legacy systems. Migration tools that rely on IMAP can selectively transfer portions of a mailbox, such as messages from specific date ranges, reducing migration time and bandwidth consumption. This approach enables a smooth transition, minimizing disruption to daily operations while IT teams complete the migration of remaining users and data.

Collaboration across hybrid environments is also improved through IMAP's compatibility with various email clients. Employees using different email clients, including Microsoft Outlook, Mozilla Thunderbird, Apple Mail, and various mobile apps, can all connect to IMAP servers regardless of whether they are hosted on-premises or in the cloud. IMAP's widespread support ensures that end users do not need to change their preferred email applications when organizations implement hybrid infrastructures, preserving user productivity and reducing the need for extensive retraining.

Hybrid environments leveraging IMAP also benefit from centralized management capabilities. System administrators can monitor mailbox activity, enforce policies, and apply security controls across both on-premises and cloud infrastructures. For example, retention policies and mailbox quotas can be applied to both environments using directory services integration and management consoles. IMAP logs from both infrastructures can be aggregated and analyzed to detect anomalies, troubleshoot synchronization issues, and ensure compliance with organizational security policies. Centralized management ensures that despite the complexity of hybrid deployments, organizations can maintain control and visibility over their entire email ecosystem.

Despite its advantages, IMAP in hybrid deployments presents certain challenges that require careful planning and maintenance. Differences in server implementations, folder naming conventions, and message size limitations between on-premises and cloud systems may lead to inconsistencies during synchronization. IMAP lacks native support for advanced collaboration features such as shared calendars, contact lists, and real-time presence information, which are common in modern cloud platforms. To address these limitations, hybrid deployments often combine IMAP with additional protocols such as CalDAV for calendar synchronization or CardDAV for contact management, enabling a more complete collaboration solution.

The ongoing rise of cloud adoption does not diminish the relevance of IMAP in hybrid environments. Instead, IMAP continues to serve as a flexible, lightweight protocol that bridges the gap between legacy and modern systems. Organizations deploying hybrid email infrastructures rely on IMAP to provide consistent mailbox access, support migration initiatives, enable secure synchronization, and maintain business continuity during transitional phases. IMAP's role as a core component of hybrid deployments allows businesses to leverage the strengths of both on-premises and cloud-based services while optimizing costs, meeting regulatory obligations, and accommodating unique operational needs.

Managing Spam and Unwanted Emails

Managing spam and unwanted emails within an IMAP-based environment is a crucial task for maintaining inbox hygiene, ensuring productivity, and safeguarding against security threats. The volume of unsolicited and potentially harmful emails continues to grow, overwhelming users and consuming valuable network and storage resources. An effective spam management strategy requires a combination of technical defenses, user training, and proactive monitoring to reduce the impact of spam on both individual users and the organization as a whole.

One of the primary methods for addressing spam is through the deployment of server-side filtering solutions. These systems, commonly referred to as spam filters or email gateways, sit between incoming mail servers and IMAP servers, scanning all inbound email traffic before it reaches the user's mailbox. These filters use a variety of techniques to identify and block spam, including content analysis, pattern recognition, and blacklisting known spam sources. Content-based filtering examines the body and headers of an email to detect common spam characteristics, such as suspicious links, known spam keywords, or unusual formatting. When combined with heuristic analysis, which evaluates the likelihood that a message is spam based on learned patterns and historical data, these filters can detect and quarantine most spam messages before they reach the IMAP server.

Another widely used technique involves the use of reputation-based filtering, where inbound emails are evaluated based on the sender's IP address and domain reputation. IPs associated with known spamming activities or frequently reported by other organizations are flagged, and messages originating from them are either blocked or routed to users' spam folders. Many organizations subscribe to global blacklists or real-time blackhole lists (RBLs), which are databases containing IP addresses of known spammers. Integrating these lists into spam filtering solutions enhances their accuracy and ensures proactive blocking of spam campaigns as they emerge.

Bayesian filtering is also employed in many spam management strategies. Bayesian filters use statistical methods to analyze incoming emails and learn from patterns based on both legitimate and spam messages. Over time, the filter refines its understanding of what constitutes spam for a particular user or organization, enabling it to make increasingly accurate decisions. Because spam patterns evolve, Bayesian filters require ongoing training, often supplemented by user feedback. When users manually mark emails as spam or not spam, this information is fed back into the filtering algorithm, improving its performance and reducing false positives or false negatives.

Despite the effectiveness of server-side filtering, some spam inevitably bypasses these systems and reaches the user's inbox. IMAP clients often incorporate client-side filtering mechanisms that provide additional protection and user control. Email clients like Outlook, Thunderbird, and Apple Mail allow users to create custom rules and filters that automatically move or delete emails based on specific criteria, such as sender address, subject line content, or message body keywords. By combining client-side filtering with server-side defenses, organizations establish a multilayered approach to spam management, reducing the burden on users while providing flexibility to tailor filters to individual needs.

Managing spam also involves implementing proper authentication protocols to verify the legitimacy of incoming emails. Techniques such as Sender Policy Framework (SPF), DomainKeys Identified Mail (DKIM), and Domain-based Message Authentication, Reporting, and Conformance (DMARC) help confirm whether a sender is authorized to send emails on behalf of a particular domain. IMAP servers integrated with these authentication protocols can check incoming messages for SPF, DKIM, and DMARC compliance, rejecting or flagging emails that fail authentication checks. This significantly reduces the risk of phishing attacks and domain spoofing, where attackers impersonate trusted senders to deceive recipients.

Quarantine management is another critical component of spam control. Rather than deleting suspected spam outright, many systems redirect them to a quarantine folder accessible to administrators or users. This allows legitimate emails misclassified as spam to be recovered while reducing the risk of important messages being permanently lost. IMAP's support for server-side folder management enables seamless integration of quarantine folders within the mailbox hierarchy, where users can review and release emails as needed. Organizations can configure automated notifications, alerting users to check their quarantines periodically to ensure no valid communication has been inadvertently blocked.

User education plays a vital role in minimizing the impact of spam and unwanted emails. Even the most advanced technical defenses cannot prevent every phishing attempt or cleverly disguised spam email from reaching users. Training employees to recognize suspicious emails, avoid clicking on unknown links, and report phishing attempts ensures an additional human layer of defense. Security awareness programs should include real-world simulations and periodic refreshers to reinforce best practices and cultivate a culture of vigilance.

Automation is increasingly utilized in managing spam and unwanted emails. Workflow automation platforms can be configured to take predefined actions based on spam detection rules. For instance, automated scripts may scan spam folders, apply additional checks such as sandboxing attachments, and notify IT teams of high-risk patterns that could indicate targeted phishing campaigns or malware distribution attempts. Automation not only improves response times but also enables rapid containment of threats before they spread across the organization.

Spam management must also consider outbound email monitoring. While the focus is often on filtering incoming spam, compromised internal accounts can be exploited by attackers to send spam from within the organization. Outbound filters inspect emails leaving the organization's network to detect and block suspicious or unauthorized activity, helping to protect the organization's domain reputation and prevent blacklisting by external mail providers.

Finally, effective spam management strategies must include regular reporting and analysis. IMAP servers and associated filtering systems generate logs detailing blocked emails, false positive rates, sender patterns, and user behavior. By analyzing this data, administrators can fine-tune filtering rules, adjust thresholds, and stay informed about emerging spam tactics. Reporting tools provide visibility into the effectiveness of spam defenses, informing decision-making and helping organizations allocate resources to further strengthen their email security posture.

By combining technical safeguards, user engagement, and automation, organizations can successfully manage spam and unwanted emails in IMAP-based environments. A layered defense not only protects against disruptive and potentially dangerous spam but also ensures that legitimate email traffic flows efficiently, supporting productivity, security, and business continuity. As spammers continue to evolve their techniques, maintaining and enhancing spam defenses will remain a crucial responsibility for IT and security teams alike.

IMAP in Enterprise Environments

IMAP plays a critical role in enterprise environments, where organizations require robust, scalable, and secure methods for managing vast volumes of email traffic across multiple departments, offices, and geographic locations. As enterprises increasingly operate in distributed and hybrid work models, IMAP serves as a foundational protocol that enables employees to access, manage, and synchronize email messages from anywhere, using a wide range of devices and email clients. The flexibility and centralized management capabilities offered by IMAP make it a key component in enterprise email infrastructures, supporting collaboration, business continuity, and compliance with regulatory requirements.

In an enterprise setting, IMAP is often deployed alongside complex infrastructures that include directory services, security appliances, load balancers, archiving systems, and collaboration platforms. The protocol's server-based architecture aligns well with enterprise needs, allowing emails to be stored centrally on mail servers and accessed remotely by users. This centralized storage approach ensures that email data remains consistent across all devices, including desktop computers, laptops, smartphones, and tablets. When employees read, move, delete, or flag messages on one device, those changes are immediately reflected across all other connected devices through IMAP synchronization, providing a seamless and consistent user experience.

Scalability is one of the core requirements in enterprise environments, and IMAP is well-suited to support large user bases. Enterprises often manage thousands or even tens of thousands of mailboxes, each containing significant volumes of email data. IMAP's efficient synchronization mechanisms, including the ability to retrieve only headers or specific portions of emails as needed, help reduce network bandwidth consumption and improve client performance. To further enhance scalability, enterprises typically deploy IMAP servers in clustered or load-balanced configurations. Load balancers distribute client requests evenly across multiple IMAP server instances, preventing server overload and ensuring that users receive prompt responses even during peak usage periods.

Security is paramount when deploying IMAP in enterprises, as email often contains sensitive information, including intellectual property, financial data, and confidential communications. IMAP servers in enterprise environments are configured to enforce TLS encryption for all client-server communications, protecting data in transit from interception and eavesdropping. In addition to transport encryption, enterprises implement strong authentication mechanisms, including multi-factor authentication (MFA) and integration with centralized identity providers such as Active Directory or LDAP. Modern enterprises increasingly rely on OAuth2 for IMAP authentication, leveraging token-based security models that reduce the risk associated with traditional password-based authentication methods.

Enterprises also face significant compliance and regulatory challenges when managing email communications. IMAP servers deployed in enterprise environments must be integrated with archival and eDiscovery systems to ensure that all email data is properly retained, indexed, and retrievable for legal, regulatory, or investigative purposes. Archiving solutions capture both incoming and outgoing emails, often in real-time, and store them in tamper-proof repositories. This ensures that organizations comply with data retention laws such as GDPR, HIPAA, and FINRA regulations. IMAP's compatibility with third-party archiving and compliance platforms allows enterprises to automate the process of preserving and managing email data across large and distributed infrastructures.

Administrative control and centralized management are crucial in enterprise IMAP deployments. Administrators require the ability to manage user accounts, enforce policies, and monitor system health across multiple servers and geographic locations. Management tools integrated with IMAP servers provide dashboards for tracking key performance indicators, such as server uptime, resource utilization, connection counts, and synchronization success rates. Additionally, detailed audit logs capture user activities, failed login attempts, message access patterns, and administrative actions, enabling security teams to detect anomalies and respond quickly to potential security incidents.

High availability and disaster recovery are fundamental components of IMAP implementations in enterprises. Enterprises typically design their IMAP infrastructure with redundancy and failover mechanisms to ensure continuous access to email services in the event of hardware failures, network outages, or natural disasters. Redundant server clusters, geographically dispersed data centers, and automated failover processes minimize downtime and maintain business continuity. Enterprises also implement regular backup schedules for email data, ensuring that mailboxes can be quickly restored from backups if data loss occurs due to system corruption, cyber-attacks, or accidental deletion.

Interoperability with collaboration tools is another important consideration for IMAP in enterprises. Modern organizations rely on a suite of productivity tools that include calendars, shared contact lists, instant messaging, document management systems, and task management platforms. IMAP servers integrate with these tools to enable smooth workflows and improve team collaboration. For example, integration with calendar applications allows meeting invitations and scheduling updates received via email to be automatically synchronized with users' calendar systems. Likewise, IMAP-based email clients often integrate with document management platforms, enabling employees to share and access files directly from within their email environment.

Enterprises also leverage IMAP automation to reduce manual workload and improve operational efficiency. Automated scripts and custom applications can be developed to interact with IMAP servers to perform routine tasks, such as automatically sorting incoming emails into designated folders, flagging important messages, archiving emails based on predefined rules, or integrating with customer relationship management (CRM) systems. Automation reduces human error, accelerates business processes, and frees up IT resources for more strategic initiatives.

With the rise of remote and hybrid work models, enterprises increasingly prioritize mobile device support in their IMAP strategies. Employees require secure, reliable access to their email accounts from various locations and devices. IMAP's device-agnostic nature ensures that employees can use a wide range of clients, including mobile apps, webmail interfaces, and traditional desktop email clients, while maintaining consistent access to their messages. Mobile device management (MDM) solutions are often employed to enforce security policies on mobile devices, including remote wipe capabilities and the enforcement of encryption for local email storage.

In enterprise environments, IMAP continues to play a vital role by providing a scalable, secure, and flexible protocol for managing email. Its ability to integrate with existing infrastructures, support compliance initiatives, and ensure reliable email access across a wide array of devices makes it an indispensable component of modern enterprise IT strategies. By optimizing IMAP deployments for performance, security, and manageability, organizations can enhance communication workflows, improve employee productivity, and safeguard their email systems against evolving operational and security challenges.

Client-side IMAP Implementations

Client-side IMAP implementations are fundamental in ensuring that users experience efficient, reliable, and seamless access to their email accounts across a variety of platforms and devices. IMAP, as a server-side protocol, provides the framework for synchronizing and managing email messages stored remotely, but it is the client-side implementation that translates IMAP commands into user-friendly interactions. Email clients that support IMAP must implement a set of core functionalities that allow users to read, compose, move, delete, and organize messages, all while ensuring these actions are accurately reflected on the server and across other connected devices. The effectiveness of an IMAP client directly impacts user productivity, mailbox performance, and overall satisfaction with the email system.

At the heart of a client-side IMAP implementation is the establishment and management of connections to the IMAP server. Clients typically initiate a TCP connection to the server and negotiate session parameters, including authentication, encryption settings, and namespace discovery. The client must handle secure communication channels, enforcing the use of Transport Layer Security (TLS) for all data transmitted between the client and server to protect user credentials and message content from eavesdropping. Additionally, robust IMAP clients must be designed to gracefully recover from connection interruptions, automatically re-establishing sessions without requiring manual user intervention and ensuring that pending synchronization tasks resume once connectivity is restored.

Authentication handling is a key aspect of client-side IMAP design. Modern IMAP clients support multiple authentication mechanisms, including traditional login-password methods and more advanced token-based systems such as OAuth2. OAuth2 integration allows IMAP clients to leverage single sign-on (SSO) platforms and comply with security standards that minimize the exposure of user passwords. Clients must also manage the lifecycle of access tokens, ensuring they are securely stored, refreshed when necessary, and revoked if compromised. Effective management of authentication flows directly impacts security and user convenience, especially in environments that enforce multi-factor authentication (MFA) policies.

Once authenticated, the client begins the synchronization process, typically by issuing the SELECT or EXAMINE commands to interact with specific folders on the server. IMAP clients must efficiently manage mailbox hierarchies, reflecting the server-side folder structure accurately and intuitively within the user interface. Client-side implementations must handle a variety of namespace conventions and delimiter characters, which can vary across IMAP servers. A key feature in this process is the ability to synchronize folder states, ensuring that any changes made on one device—such as renaming a folder or moving messages between folders—are propagated to the server and subsequently reflected on all other connected devices.

Message fetching is a core functionality in client-side IMAP implementations. IMAP supports selective fetching of message components, allowing clients to download only the headers, specific parts of the message body, or entire messages as needed. This capability is essential for optimizing performance and reducing bandwidth consumption, particularly in environments with limited network resources or when dealing with large mailboxes. Clients must intelligently manage fetching strategies based on user behavior. For example, a client may initially display message headers in a list view and only retrieve the full message content and attachments when a user opens the message. More advanced clients support partial fetching techniques, retrieving only a portion of a large message and providing the user with an option to download the remainder if desired.

Client-side IMAP implementations also manage the handling of message flags and attributes. IMAP defines standard flags such as \Seen, \Answered, \Flagged, \Deleted, and \Draft, which reflect the status of messages within the mailbox. The client must provide intuitive methods for users to apply or remove these flags, such as marking a message as read or flagging it for follow-up, and then issue the appropriate STORE or UID STORE commands to synchronize these changes with the server. Clients may also support custom flags and labels, allowing users to apply personalized tags to messages for enhanced organization and retrieval.

Another vital component of client-side IMAP design is search functionality. The IMAP SEARCH command enables clients to query messages based on various criteria, including sender, recipient, subject, date range, and content keywords. Effective clients offer user-friendly search interfaces that abstract the complexity of constructing IMAP search queries, while also supporting advanced filtering options. Some implementations offload search tasks to the server to leverage server-side indexing and reduce client resource consumption, while others perform local indexing to enable faster searches on previously synchronized messages. Balancing between server-side and client-side search capabilities is crucial for delivering a responsive and efficient search experience.

Client-side IMAP implementations must also manage message composition and sending, which typically involves integration with the Simple Mail Transfer Protocol (SMTP). When users compose and send messages through their IMAP client, the client is responsible for transmitting the message via SMTP while simultaneously saving a copy to the Sent folder on the IMAP server using the APPEND command. This ensures consistency across devices and allows users to view their sent messages from any connected client.

Offline functionality is another key feature in client-side IMAP applications. To provide uninterrupted access to email when network connectivity is unavailable, IMAP clients often cache synchronized messages and folders locally. Offline capabilities enable users to read, compose, and organize emails without an active connection, with changes automatically synchronized to the server once the client reconnects. Effective offline caching requires efficient local storage management, ensuring that cached data is encrypted, that cache sizes are configurable, and that obsolete or unnecessary data is periodically purged to conserve storage space.

In addition to core IMAP features, modern clients incorporate user experience enhancements, such as conversation or threaded views, which group related messages into coherent discussions. This feature, while implemented client-side, relies on accurate parsing of email headers such as In-Reply-To and References to link messages within a thread. Clients may also integrate with calendar systems, contact managers, and productivity tools, enabling users to schedule events or manage tasks directly from within the email application.

Performance optimization and resource management are essential for client-side IMAP applications, particularly when operating in environments with constrained resources such as mobile devices. Clients must minimize memory usage, optimize synchronization intervals, and reduce the frequency of polling the server for changes to conserve battery life and network bandwidth. Additionally, clients must provide configurable settings, allowing users or administrators to adjust synchronization behaviors, such as limiting synchronization to certain folders, restricting the download of attachments on mobile networks, or defining retention periods for cached messages.

Client-side IMAP implementations serve as the critical interface between end users and remote email systems. By effectively managing authentication, synchronization, message handling, search functionality, and offline access, IMAP clients deliver a seamless and secure email experience across diverse platforms and devices. The success of an IMAP deployment often hinges on the quality and performance of its client-side implementation, which must balance technical robustness with user-centric design principles to meet the evolving demands of modern email communication.

Server-side IMAP Implementations

Server-side IMAP implementations are the backbone of modern email systems, providing centralized storage, access, and management of email messages for users across diverse networks and devices. An IMAP server is responsible for hosting user mailboxes, handling client requests, enforcing security policies, and ensuring the integrity and availability of email data. Unlike client-side implementations that focus on user interaction and interface design, server-side IMAP implementations are engineered for performance, scalability, and reliability in handling concurrent connections and vast amounts of data.

At its core, a server-side IMAP implementation listens for client connections on designated ports, typically 143 for plaintext or STARTTLS and 993 for implicit TLS connections. Upon establishing a connection, the server authenticates the client using supported methods such as LOGIN, CRAM-MD5, or more advanced mechanisms like OAuth2. A well-designed IMAP server must offer flexibility in authentication to meet the security and regulatory requirements of various organizations. The server must also enforce encryption via TLS to protect user credentials and message data during transit.

Once authentication is successful, the IMAP server allows the client to interact with the user's mailbox. A core responsibility of the server-side implementation is the efficient management of folders and message hierarchies. The server maintains the complete structure of folders, including standard ones like Inbox, Sent, Trash, Drafts, and user-created folders. IMAP servers often support both personal and shared folders, with namespace configurations that define how these folders are accessed and displayed by clients. The server handles folder creation, deletion, renaming, and subscription requests, ensuring synchronization of changes across all connected devices.

Message storage and retrieval are at the heart of IMAP server functionality. Messages are stored on the server in a structured format, often in file-based storage systems such as the Maildir format or within database-backed systems. The server is responsible for indexing and retrieving messages efficiently, especially when clients request large volumes of emails or when executing search queries. A high-performance IMAP server implementation includes mechanisms for indexing message headers, body content, and metadata to expedite search and filtering operations. The FETCH command, which clients use to retrieve messages, is processed by the server with options to deliver full messages, headers only, or specific parts of a message, such as attachments or plain text bodies.

IMAP servers also manage message flags and attributes, which represent the status of individual emails. These flags include standard IMAP flags such as \Seen, \Answered, \Flagged, \Deleted, and \Draft. The server must track and update these flags as clients issue STORE or UID STORE commands to mark messages as read, flagged, or deleted. These changes must be immediately reflected on the server and propagated to all connected clients to maintain consistency. Some IMAP server implementations also support user-defined flags, providing additional flexibility for advanced categorization or integration with third-party systems.

Scalability is a defining feature of robust server-side IMAP implementations. Enterprises often rely on IMAP servers to manage thousands of mailboxes and millions of messages simultaneously. To handle this demand, IMAP servers are designed to operate in distributed or clustered environments, with load balancers distributing client requests across multiple server nodes. The server architecture must ensure that mailbox data remains consistent and synchronized across nodes, often leveraging shared storage or replication mechanisms. High-availability configurations are common, with redundant servers providing failover capabilities in the event of hardware or network failures.

Security is another cornerstone of server-side IMAP design. In addition to TLS encryption and secure authentication, IMAP servers must enforce access control policies that restrict user permissions based on roles or organizational policies. For example, shared mailboxes may have different access levels, allowing some users to read-only while granting others full modification rights. IMAP servers also integrate with directory services such as LDAP or Active Directory to centralize user management and authentication. Integration with email security gateways allows IMAP servers to cooperate with antispam and antivirus solutions, ensuring that malicious emails are filtered before they reach user mailboxes.

Resource management is essential for optimizing server performance. IMAP servers must carefully manage memory usage, disk I/O, and CPU resources to handle spikes in concurrent connections and heavy workloads. Techniques such as connection pooling, efficient thread management, and asynchronous I/O processing are commonly employed to improve server responsiveness. The server may also implement quota management, restricting mailbox sizes to prevent individual accounts from consuming disproportionate amounts of storage resources.

Advanced server-side IMAP implementations offer support for extensions that enhance functionality and performance. For example, the IMAP IDLE extension allows the server to maintain an open connection with clients, notifying them immediately when new messages arrive, reducing the need for frequent polling. Other extensions include CONDSTORE and QRESYNC, which optimize synchronization by minimizing the amount of data exchanged during resynchronization processes. These extensions are especially valuable in environments with mobile clients or large mailboxes, where bandwidth and latency considerations are critical.

Server-side logging and monitoring are crucial for administrators to maintain visibility into IMAP server operations. Logs capture detailed information about client connections, authentication events, mailbox transactions, and errors. This information is essential for troubleshooting issues, auditing access, and detecting anomalies that may indicate security breaches or system malfunctions. Monitoring tools integrated with IMAP servers provide real-time insights into server health, connection counts, resource usage, and performance metrics, enabling administrators to proactively address potential problems.

Backup and disaster recovery mechanisms are integral to IMAP server environments. Since the IMAP server is the central repository for user emails, ensuring that mailbox data is regularly backed up and easily recoverable is vital. Server-side backup strategies may include snapshot-based file system backups, replication to secondary storage systems, or integration with enterprise backup solutions. Recovery procedures must be tested and documented to guarantee that mailboxes can be restored quickly in the event of data loss or system failure.

Customization and extensibility are often necessary in enterprise-grade IMAP server deployments. Organizations may require specialized hooks or plugins to integrate IMAP servers with other enterprise systems, such as customer relationship management (CRM) platforms, ticketing systems, or compliance solutions. Open-source IMAP servers, such as Dovecot or Cyrus IMAP, provide flexible architectures that allow developers to extend functionality through scripting or module development, supporting unique business needs or regulatory requirements.

A successful server-side IMAP implementation ensures that email remains a reliable and secure communication channel for users. By providing efficient mailbox management, high performance under load, and robust security features, the IMAP server is a vital component of modern IT infrastructures. Whether deployed on-premises, in hybrid environments, or as part of a managed cloud service, server-side IMAP continues to serve as a critical enabler of global email communication and collaboration.

User Experience and IMAP Clients

The user experience in IMAP clients is a critical factor that influences how effectively individuals and organizations interact with their email systems. While IMAP serves as the backend protocol that governs how email data is retrieved, stored, and synchronized with remote servers, it is the client-side implementation that determines how seamlessly and intuitively users can manage their communications. A well-designed IMAP client should provide a fast, responsive, and consistent user experience, regardless of the device or platform being used, while effectively abstracting the complexity of the IMAP protocol itself.

The first and most noticeable component of the user experience in IMAP clients is the interface design. The graphical user interface (GUI) must balance simplicity with functionality, allowing users to access essential features without overwhelming them with unnecessary complexity. Folder structures, inbox views, and message previews must be logically arranged, offering users clear visibility into their emails. Effective clients ensure that core actions such as reading, replying, forwarding, archiving, and deleting messages are easily accessible. Many modern IMAP clients provide customizable interfaces that allow users to personalize the layout, select preferred color schemes, adjust font sizes, and configure how message threads are displayed.

Synchronization speed and accuracy are key aspects that shape user satisfaction with IMAP clients. Since IMAP synchronizes data between the server and the client, users expect real-time updates across all devices. For instance, when a message is read, moved to a folder, or marked as important on one device, the change should be reflected instantly on other connected devices. Laggy synchronization or inconsistencies between devices lead to frustration and can negatively affect productivity. Well-optimized IMAP clients implement intelligent synchronization algorithms that minimize bandwidth usage while ensuring changes are propagated quickly and reliably.

IMAP clients also play a vital role in offline access and caching, which are essential for users who frequently work in environments with limited or intermittent internet connectivity. A smooth offline experience depends on how effectively the client downloads and caches messages and attachments locally. Some clients allow users to configure offline settings, such as selecting which folders to synchronize, defining the time period for cached emails, or setting limits on attachment downloads based on file size or network type. Providing users with access to their most recent and relevant emails offline ensures continuous workflow, even when disconnected from the IMAP server.

Search functionality is another major factor influencing the overall user experience. Users expect the ability to quickly locate emails based on a variety of criteria, including sender, recipient, subject, keywords, dates, and message content. The efficiency of the search experience largely depends on whether the client leverages server-side search capabilities or relies on locally indexed data. Clients that integrate with the IMAP SEARCH command can perform server-side searches across large mailboxes without downloading entire folders, optimizing performance for users working with cloud-based or remote servers. At the same time, clients may offer local search options to quickly retrieve cached messages. Providing both server-side and local search functionality ensures that users can efficiently locate information in different network and storage scenarios.

Modern IMAP clients must also support threaded conversations, which group related emails into single discussions based on headers like In-Reply-To and References. This feature significantly improves readability and organization by presenting conversations in a hierarchical structure that makes it easier to follow message flows. Clients that offer flexible threading options, such as collapsing or expanding threads, filtering based on participants, or visually distinguishing between different conversation branches, provide users with greater control over how they navigate their inboxes.

A seamless user experience also depends on the integration of IMAP clients with productivity and collaboration tools. Many IMAP clients integrate with calendar applications, contact managers, and third-party task management systems, enabling users to schedule events, manage contacts, and create tasks directly from their inboxes. These integrations reduce the need for users to switch between applications, streamlining workflows and improving efficiency. For example, when a user receives an email containing a meeting invitation, a well-integrated IMAP client can automatically parse the message and allow the user to add the event to their calendar with a single click.

The handling of attachments within IMAP clients is another area that greatly impacts user satisfaction. Efficient clients provide intuitive options for downloading, previewing, and sharing attachments. They may also offer integrations with cloud storage services, allowing users to save attachments directly to platforms like Google Drive, Dropbox, or OneDrive without downloading them to local storage. Furthermore, modern clients often include automatic attachment management settings that help users control storage usage by defining retention periods or setting limits for automatic downloads on mobile networks.

Security features incorporated into IMAP clients also contribute to the overall user experience by providing peace of mind and reinforcing safe communication practices. Clients must support encryption standards such as TLS to secure IMAP connections and should offer options for end-to-end encryption using protocols like PGP or S/MIME. Additionally, well-designed clients implement phishing and spam detection mechanisms, alerting users to suspicious emails and helping them avoid potential security threats.

Mobile IMAP clients require particular attention to usability, given the limitations of smaller screens and touch-based interfaces. Mobile clients must deliver all the critical functionalities of their desktop counterparts while optimizing the layout and navigation for smartphones and tablets. Features such as swipe gestures for archiving or deleting emails, push notifications for new messages, and compact threading views are essential for maintaining efficiency and convenience on mobile devices. Clients must also be optimized for battery and data efficiency, ensuring minimal resource consumption without sacrificing responsiveness or synchronization speed.

Customization and personalization options enhance the user experience by allowing individuals to tailor the client's behavior to their preferences. Advanced IMAP clients provide a wide range of settings, including custom keyboard shortcuts, configurable sync schedules, notification controls, and display options. This flexibility empowers users to create workflows that align with their specific needs, whether they are power users managing multiple accounts and folders or casual users focused on a single inbox.

Ultimately, the quality of a client-side IMAP implementation is measured by how effectively it bridges the gap between the technical operation of the IMAP protocol and the everyday needs of its users. A positive user experience in IMAP clients hinges on responsiveness, reliability, ease of use, and seamless integration with other tools and systems. By prioritizing intuitive design, robust synchronization, and performance optimization, IMAP clients ensure that users can manage their communications effectively in today's fast-paced, multi-device environments.

Open Source IMAP Solutions

Open source IMAP solutions play a crucial role in providing organizations and developers with flexible, customizable, and cost-effective email infrastructure options. Unlike proprietary email servers, open source IMAP servers offer transparency, community-driven development, and the freedom to tailor functionality according to specific organizational or project requirements. Many enterprises, small businesses, and service providers choose open source IMAP servers to gain greater control over their email systems, enhance security, and avoid vendor lock-in. These solutions are widely deployed in a variety of environments, ranging from small-scale mail systems to large-scale distributed architectures supporting millions of users.

One of the most widely adopted open source IMAP servers is Dovecot. Known for its performance, simplicity, and security, Dovecot is highly regarded within the open source community and enterprise sectors alike. Dovecot's modular architecture allows administrators to enable or disable specific components, tailoring the system to the organization's needs. It supports a broad range of authentication mechanisms, including PAM, LDAP, SQL databases, and OAuth2, making it compatible with diverse identity management systems. Dovecot's native support for mail storage formats such as Maildir and mbox, combined with its ability to scale in clustered configurations, has made it a default choice for many Linux distributions and internet service providers (ISPs) seeking a reliable IMAP solution.

Cyrus IMAP is another robust open source IMAP server that emphasizes scalability and advanced functionality. Developed by Carnegie Mellon University, Cyrus IMAP is often used in enterprise environments that require fine-grained control over email data and high-performance processing. Unlike traditional IMAP servers, Cyrus employs a sealed server model, where mailbox data is managed entirely on the server side without granting clients direct access to the underlying filesystem. This architecture enhances security and allows for efficient mailbox indexing and access. Cyrus IMAP supports advanced features such as server-side email filtering through the Sieve scripting language, shared mailboxes, quotas, and access control lists (ACLs) for collaborative email environments. Its support for clustering and replication ensures high availability and load balancing in mission-critical deployments.

Courier IMAP is another longstanding open source IMAP server solution, popular for its lightweight design and ease of integration with other mail services, such as the Courier Mail Server. Courier IMAP supports both Maildir and mbox storage formats and is known for its compatibility with a wide variety of IMAP clients. Its relatively simple configuration files and resource-friendly footprint make it suitable for smaller-scale deployments or environments with limited system resources. Despite being less feature-rich compared to Dovecot or Cyrus, Courier IMAP remains a viable option for administrators seeking a straightforward and dependable IMAP implementation.

One of the key benefits of open source IMAP solutions is the ability to fully inspect and modify the source code. This transparency fosters trust by allowing organizations to verify that no hidden functionality, such as backdoors or data collection mechanisms, exists within the software. Moreover, organizations with in-house development teams can customize the IMAP server to suit their unique operational requirements. For example, they might introduce bespoke authentication workflows, integrate with proprietary systems, or develop specialized logging and reporting features tailored to their compliance needs.

Open source IMAP servers typically enjoy active community support and ongoing development. Global communities of contributors continually audit the codebase for security vulnerabilities, release timely patches, and collaborate on new features that reflect emerging industry trends. This community-driven model accelerates innovation and ensures that open source IMAP servers evolve alongside the changing needs of modern email infrastructures. Documentation, tutorials, forums, and mailing lists further enrich the user experience by providing valuable resources for troubleshooting, optimization, and implementation guidance.

Security is a primary focus in open source IMAP solutions. Most servers support industry-standard encryption protocols, such as TLS, to secure communications between clients and servers. They also integrate with various authentication backends and allow for the enforcement of strong password policies, multi-factor authentication, and account lockout mechanisms. Administrators can implement fail2ban or similar intrusion prevention tools to monitor IMAP logs and automatically block suspicious IP addresses exhibiting brute-force attack patterns. Furthermore, the open development model ensures that security vulnerabilities are often identified and addressed more quickly compared to closed-source alternatives, reducing the risk of long-term exposure.

In terms of performance, open source IMAP servers are designed to handle high concurrency and large mailbox sizes efficiently. Dovecot, for instance, utilizes efficient indexing mechanisms and supports IMAP extensions such as CONDSTORE and QRESYNC to optimize synchronization processes, reducing server load and improving client responsiveness. These features are essential in environments where users access their mailboxes from multiple devices, requiring real-time updates and efficient handling of large volumes of email traffic.

Another strength of open source IMAP solutions is their interoperability with other open source email components. IMAP servers are often deployed alongside open source SMTP servers, such as Postfix or Exim, and integrated with antispam and antivirus tools like SpamAssassin and ClamAV. Combined, these components form complete email ecosystems capable of meeting the demands of enterprise environments without incurring the licensing fees associated with commercial products. Additionally, open source webmail clients like Roundcube or RainLoop are commonly paired with IMAP servers to provide users with intuitive, browser-based access to their mailboxes.

Deployment flexibility is another hallmark of open source IMAP solutions. Administrators can deploy IMAP servers on a variety of operating systems, including major Linux distributions, BSD variants, and even containers in cloud-native environments using platforms such as Kubernetes or Docker. Containerization of IMAP services enables rapid deployment, simplified scaling, and improved isolation between services. Furthermore, open source IMAP servers can be deployed in hybrid or cloud environments, supporting organizations that require a mix of on-premises and cloud-hosted infrastructure.

Cost savings are an undeniable advantage of adopting open source IMAP servers. By eliminating licensing fees and allowing for customization without vendor-imposed restrictions, organizations can allocate resources more efficiently toward hardware, support, or other mission-critical services. This is particularly appealing to startups, educational institutions, and non-profits operating under tight budget constraints, as well as large enterprises seeking to reduce their total cost of ownership.

Open source IMAP solutions continue to thrive as trusted components of modern email infrastructures. Their emphasis on security, performance, flexibility, and community collaboration ensures that organizations have access to powerful and adaptable tools for managing email communications. By choosing open source IMAP servers, businesses gain autonomy over their email systems, the ability to innovate freely, and the confidence that their infrastructure is built on transparent and well-supported software.

IMAP Testing and Validation

IMAP testing and validation are critical processes in ensuring the reliability, security, and performance of IMAP-based email systems. As IMAP serves as the backbone protocol for remote email access, administrators and developers must thoroughly test IMAP servers and clients to identify configuration issues, interoperability problems, or performance bottlenecks before deployment and during ongoing operations. A structured approach to IMAP testing ensures that users experience a stable, responsive, and secure email service, regardless of the scale or complexity of the environment.

The first step in IMAP testing typically involves validating the basic connectivity between the client and server. This foundational test ensures that the server is listening on the correct IMAP ports, typically port 143 for plaintext or STARTTLS connections and port 993 for implicit TLS. Administrators use tools such as Telnet, OpenSSL, or Netcat to initiate raw IMAP sessions and verify that the server responds with the appropriate greeting message. These basic connectivity tests confirm that the server is reachable over the network and that firewall rules and network configurations permit IMAP traffic to flow correctly between clients and servers.

Once basic connectivity is established, the next stage involves authentication testing. IMAP servers must support multiple authentication mechanisms, such as plaintext LOGIN, CRAM-MD5, or modern OAuth2 token-based authentication. Comprehensive testing validates that each supported mechanism works as intended and that the server enforces appropriate security measures, such as rejecting plaintext authentication attempts unless encrypted channels are used. Automated tools like imaptest, imap-login-tools, or custom scripts simulate authentication workflows to ensure that valid credentials are accepted, invalid credentials are rejected, and account lockout policies are correctly enforced after repeated failed login attempts.

TLS validation is another crucial aspect of IMAP testing. Ensuring that the IMAP server enforces secure communication is paramount to protecting data in transit. Tests must confirm that TLS certificates are correctly installed, valid, and signed by a trusted certificate authority. Validation includes checking the cipher suites used by the server to ensure they meet current security standards and verifying that the server does not permit outdated or vulnerable protocols such as SSLv3 or weak ciphers. Security scanners like SSL Labs, testssl.sh, or OpenSSL commands provide valuable insights into the strength and correctness of the server's TLS configuration.

Functional testing of IMAP commands is the next layer of validation. IMAP servers must correctly handle the full suite of IMAP commands, including LOGIN, SELECT, FETCH, STORE, APPEND, SEARCH, COPY, and LOGOUT. Test scripts and IMAP clients are used to verify that these commands produce the expected server responses and that mailbox operations perform as intended. For example, tests might validate that a FETCH command correctly retrieves message headers or bodies, that a STORE command successfully marks a message as read, or that an APPEND command stores new messages in the specified folder. These tests ensure the server adheres to the IMAP protocol specifications and provides consistent behavior to different clients.

Interoperability testing is essential, especially in environments where users connect to the IMAP server from various clients, including Outlook, Thunderbird, Apple Mail, mobile apps, and webmail interfaces. Different IMAP clients sometimes interpret the IMAP protocol differently or rely on specific extensions such as IDLE, CONDSTORE, or QRESYNC. Testing with a variety of clients ensures that all features, including folder synchronization, message flag handling, and threading, work correctly across platforms. It also helps uncover discrepancies in how different clients handle namespaces, delimiter characters, or non-standard IMAP extensions, which could impact the user experience.

Performance testing forms a critical component of IMAP validation, particularly in enterprise environments with thousands of concurrent users. Load testing tools like imaptest or JMeter with IMAP plugins simulate large numbers of concurrent connections, mailbox synchronizations, and message fetches to assess the server's performance under stress. These tests help identify potential performance bottlenecks related to CPU usage, memory consumption, disk I/O, or network bandwidth limitations. Based on the test results, administrators can fine-tune server parameters, such as connection limits, thread pools, and caching settings, to optimize the IMAP service for production workloads.

IMAP servers must also be tested for resilience and failover scenarios. These tests simulate unexpected events such as network outages, server crashes, or storage failures to verify that the IMAP service recovers gracefully and that client sessions can reconnect without data loss. For example, in a clustered IMAP deployment, failover tests confirm that when a primary node becomes unavailable, load balancers successfully route client connections to secondary nodes and that mailbox synchronization resumes correctly once service is restored. Recovery testing helps validate the robustness of high availability configurations and ensures that business continuity objectives are met.

Security testing is equally important in IMAP environments. In addition to validating encryption and authentication, penetration testing techniques are used to assess the server's exposure to common attack vectors, such as IMAP injection attacks, brute-force login attempts, or denial-of-service (DoS) vulnerabilities. Tools like Hydra and Medusa can simulate credential brute-force attempts to confirm that intrusion detection and prevention systems respond appropriately. Administrators may also conduct fuzz testing, where the IMAP server is bombarded with malformed or unexpected input to identify potential crashes, memory leaks, or buffer overflow vulnerabilities that could be exploited by attackers.

Monitoring and log validation play a critical role in the testing and validation process. IMAP servers generate extensive logs that capture connection attempts, authentication successes and failures, command execution, and error messages. Testing should confirm that logs are correctly generated, timestamped, and include sufficient detail for troubleshooting and auditing. Additionally, administrators must validate that monitoring tools, such as Prometheus or Nagios, accurately capture metrics related to IMAP server health, including connection counts, latency, and resource usage. This ensures that administrators can detect anomalies in real time and respond proactively to emerging issues.

Regression testing is another important practice in IMAP validation. Whenever changes are made to the IMAP server software, such as upgrades, configuration adjustments, or integration of new plugins, thorough regression tests must be conducted to ensure that previously functioning features remain operational. Automated regression testing frameworks reduce the time and effort required to perform repetitive validation tasks, helping teams maintain confidence in system stability while accelerating development and deployment cycles.

IMAP testing and validation provide essential safeguards against system failures, security risks, and degraded user experiences. By thoroughly testing connectivity, functionality, security, and performance, organizations ensure that their IMAP services deliver high reliability and meet both technical and business expectations. The comprehensive approach to testing not only protects against costly outages but also supports long-term operational excellence by maintaining a robust, secure, and user-friendly email infrastructure.

Future Trends in IMAP

As email continues to be a critical component of both personal and business communication, the Internet Message Access Protocol (IMAP) remains a vital technology underpinning modern email systems. However, IMAP, originally designed in the 1980s, must now evolve to meet the demands of today's rapidly changing technological landscape. The future of IMAP is shaped by trends such as cloud-native deployments, tighter security standards, automation, integration with emerging collaboration tools, and the growing need for enhanced user experiences. These trends point to IMAP evolving beyond its traditional role, positioning it as a flexible component of increasingly complex digital ecosystems.

One significant trend is the continued shift toward cloud-native infrastructure. More organizations are migrating IMAP workloads from traditional on-premises servers to cloud platforms, where they benefit from scalability, resiliency, and ease of management. In this context, IMAP servers are increasingly containerized and deployed using orchestration platforms like Kubernetes. This approach allows for dynamic scaling of IMAP services to meet varying loads and ensures high availability across geographically distributed regions. As enterprises adopt hybrid and multi-cloud strategies, IMAP services will need to integrate more seamlessly with cloud-native authentication systems, logging platforms, and monitoring tools, further blurring the line between traditional IMAP environments and modern cloud ecosystems.

Another notable trend shaping IMAP's future is the push for enhanced security. In response to the ever-increasing number of cyber threats targeting email systems, IMAP is increasingly being integrated with modern authentication frameworks like OAuth2 and OpenID Connect. These mechanisms reduce the reliance on static username and password combinations by introducing token-based authentication models that are less susceptible to brute-force attacks or credential theft. Additionally, future IMAP implementations will likely mandate encryption for all connections by default, further solidifying TLS as a required standard rather than an optional feature. Security-related extensions such as Channel Binding (RFC 5056) may also gain broader adoption to further fortify IMAP sessions against man-in-the-middle attacks and session hijacking.

The role of IMAP in automation and artificial intelligence-driven workflows is also expected to expand. As organizations seek to streamline processes and reduce manual intervention, IMAP will increasingly be used in conjunction with workflow automation platforms, robotic process automation (RPA) tools, and artificial intelligence systems. For example, future integrations may include AI-powered systems that automatically parse incoming emails, extract structured data, and trigger downstream actions such as updating CRM records, initiating support tickets, or filing compliance documentation. IMAP's flexibility makes it well-suited for serving as a data input layer for automated systems, feeding email content into advanced analytics and machine learning models.

User experience improvements also shape the trajectory of IMAP's evolution. Modern users expect instant, seamless access to their emails across devices and platforms, and IMAP will need to adapt to meet these expectations more effectively. Although the IMAP IDLE command currently enables near-real-time push notifications, further optimizations are likely to emerge to reduce latency and enhance synchronization efficiency. Lightweight synchronization mechanisms, more efficient data streaming capabilities, and better offline support will likely be incorporated into IMAP clients and servers to deliver faster and smoother user experiences, particularly in mobile and bandwidth-constrained environments.

In parallel with these trends, the convergence of email and collaboration platforms will continue to influence how IMAP is leveraged. As teams increasingly rely on integrated collaboration suites that blend email, chat, file sharing, and task management, IMAP will need to coexist with APIs from platforms like Microsoft Teams, Slack, Google Workspace, and others. This convergence may lead to IMAP being used primarily as a transport mechanism for email data while higher-level integrations present messages as part of broader collaborative workflows. For example, an email retrieved via IMAP could be automatically converted into a collaborative document comment, a shared task, or a real-time chat thread, extending the functionality of traditional inboxes beyond conventional email.

There is also an increasing focus on data privacy and regulatory compliance in IMAP ecosystems. As global regulations like GDPR, CCPA, and other regional privacy frameworks expand, IMAP servers will need to incorporate features that facilitate compliance. This includes support for automated data retention policies, message expiration capabilities, and the ability to easily export and delete personal data upon user request. IMAP solutions may also integrate with compliance monitoring systems and data loss prevention (DLP) tools, enabling organizations to scan email content for sensitive information and enforce policies designed to protect confidential data.

Open standards and interoperability will continue to play a role in shaping IMAP's future. The protocol's longevity is partly due to its wide acceptance and ability to operate with a broad range of email clients and servers. However, new RFCs and extensions will likely be introduced to modernize IMAP's capabilities further. Developers may work to address known limitations, such as improving support for shared folders and access control lists, optimizing synchronization for very large mailboxes, or introducing more efficient message compression techniques. Community-driven development, supported by organizations and open-source contributors, will ensure that IMAP remains adaptable and relevant as email technologies evolve.

The integration of IMAP with emerging technologies such as blockchain and decentralized identity systems may also become more common in niche applications. These technologies could be used to enhance email security, provide immutable audit trails for critical communications, or introduce new methods of verifying sender authenticity. While such use cases may initially be experimental or limited to specific industries, they reflect a broader trend of integrating IMAP with next-generation security and data integrity frameworks.

Finally, the future of IMAP will continue to be shaped by the growing demand for analytics and business intelligence derived from email data. IMAP servers and clients may increasingly include features that allow for the collection and analysis of metadata, such as message flow patterns, response times, and communication trends. By aggregating and visualizing this data, organizations can gain insights into team productivity, customer service effectiveness, and operational bottlenecks, turning email systems into valuable sources of business intelligence.

In this evolving landscape, IMAP remains a foundational technology that will continue to adapt and integrate with modern communication ecosystems. The trends shaping IMAP's future highlight the need for flexibility, security, interoperability, and intelligent automation. As organizations seek to modernize their email infrastructure while meeting the demands of increasingly distributed workforces, IMAP will persist as a vital link between traditional email workflows and the broader digital workplace of the future.

IMAP and AI: Intelligent Email Management

The integration of IMAP with artificial intelligence is redefining the way email is managed, processed, and optimized across modern organizations. IMAP, as a protocol, has long been the backbone for accessing and synchronizing email messages across multiple devices and platforms. However, when combined with AI-driven systems, IMAP's role is elevated from simple data synchronization to powering intelligent email management processes that enhance productivity, automate repetitive tasks, and deliver more meaningful user experiences. The fusion of AI and IMAP creates an environment where traditional email workflows become more dynamic, adaptive, and efficient, particularly as the volume and complexity of email communications continue to grow exponentially.

One of the most impactful ways AI enhances IMAP environments is through automated email classification and prioritization. AI-powered systems can analyze incoming messages retrieved via IMAP and categorize them based on content, sender behavior, tone, and historical interaction patterns. By employing natural language processing and machine learning models, these systems can distinguish between high-priority messages, such as client requests or urgent team communications, and lower-priority emails, such as newsletters or automated notifications. This intelligent classification allows users to focus on what matters most without manually sorting through a cluttered inbox. For example, an AI-enhanced IMAP workflow might automatically flag emails from key clients as urgent and route them to a designated folder or highlight them within the user interface.

AI's role in intelligent email management also extends to smart response generation. Leveraging machine learning and deep learning models trained on past correspondence, AI systems integrated with IMAP clients can suggest contextually appropriate replies to emails. These smart replies accelerate response times and ensure communication consistency across teams. In customer service environments, AI can analyze incoming support requests and recommend or draft initial responses for review by human agents, reducing the time needed to address common queries. Over time, AI models refine their suggestions based on user feedback, becoming more accurate and personalized.

Email summarization is another area where AI delivers significant value. With the rise of information overload, users often struggle to process lengthy emails or threads with multiple responses. AI models can process the content of emails fetched via IMAP and generate concise summaries that capture the key points, action items, and decisions discussed within the message. These summaries save time, particularly for executives or project managers who need to stay informed without reviewing every detail. AI-powered summarization tools can also present key takeaways in dashboard formats, providing an at-a-glance view of critical communications from large email volumes.

AI's analytical capabilities further enhance IMAP-driven email workflows by enabling sentiment analysis. Sentiment detection models can assess the tone and emotional context of incoming messages, helping organizations understand customer satisfaction or identify potential issues before they escalate. For example, an AI system might flag emails with negative sentiment from customers, prompting customer service teams to prioritize resolution. Sentiment analysis can also be used internally, helping managers gauge team morale based on internal communications and guiding leadership strategies accordingly.

In the realm of security and compliance, AI significantly augments traditional IMAP environments. AI-driven anomaly detection systems can continuously analyze patterns in email traffic, identifying suspicious behavior such as phishing attempts, unauthorized access to IMAP accounts, or unusual login locations. These systems go beyond static rule-based filters by learning from normal user behavior and detecting deviations that may indicate security incidents. AI-enhanced security mechanisms integrated with IMAP can proactively quarantine suspect messages, block fraudulent login attempts, and alert security teams in real time.

Automation is at the core of AI's value proposition when combined with IMAP. AI-powered workflow automation platforms can process emails retrieved via IMAP and trigger downstream actions without human intervention. For example, AI systems can extract data from invoices attached to emails, validate the information against existing records, and automatically input the data into financial or ERP systems. In legal or compliance departments, AI can analyze contract-related emails and auto-tag documents according to regulatory requirements. By eliminating manual tasks, AI-driven automation significantly reduces operational costs and minimizes human error.

AI also plays a growing role in enhancing search and discovery capabilities within IMAP environments. Traditional IMAP search functions rely on matching specific keywords or metadata fields, which can be limiting when users need to find information buried deep within message bodies or attachments. AI-powered semantic search engines, integrated into IMAP clients, allow users to conduct more intuitive and context-aware searches. These systems understand natural language queries and retrieve relevant emails based on the meaning of the query rather than exact keyword matches. As a result, users can locate critical information more quickly, improving efficiency and reducing frustration.

Beyond search, AI can also contribute to intelligent folder management. By analyzing user behavior and communication patterns, AI models can recommend folder structures or even automatically create and organize folders. For instance, if a user frequently receives project-related emails from multiple stakeholders, the AI system might suggest creating a new project folder and automatically route related emails to it. Over time, these recommendations adapt as user workflows change, ensuring that the organization of the inbox evolves alongside shifting priorities and responsibilities.

The integration of AI with IMAP is also reshaping mobile email experiences. Mobile IMAP clients often face constraints related to screen size, battery life, and bandwidth. AI can optimize the mobile email experience by predicting which emails are most likely to require immediate attention and preloading those messages and attachments in the background. AI-driven mobile clients can also adjust synchronization frequencies based on user patterns, conserving device resources without sacrificing performance.

Additionally, AI models can assist in enhancing accessibility within IMAP clients. Speech-to-text and text-to-speech capabilities allow visually impaired users to compose or listen to emails with greater ease. AI can also suggest simplified versions of complex messages, making content more accessible to users with cognitive disabilities or those operating in high-distraction environments.

As organizations seek to streamline communication workflows and increase responsiveness, the combination of IMAP and AI emerges as a powerful solution. This synergy allows for intelligent email management systems that go beyond traditional filtering and synchronization to deliver personalized, efficient, and automated experiences. As AI models continue to advance, IMAP-powered platforms will increasingly offer features that anticipate user needs, automate routine tasks, and provide actionable insights, transforming email from a passive communication tool into an active driver of business productivity and decision-making.

Customizing IMAP Deployments

Customizing IMAP deployments is a vital practice for organizations seeking to align their email infrastructure with unique business requirements, security policies, and operational workflows. IMAP, as a protocol, is highly adaptable and can be tailored at both the server and client levels to meet specific organizational demands. While the default behavior of IMAP servers offers sufficient functionality for many standard environments, enterprises with specialized needs often go beyond the default configurations to optimize performance, enhance security, integrate with custom tools, and create a seamless user experience.

One of the key areas where customization plays a role is in defining the storage backend of the IMAP server. By default, many IMAP servers such as Dovecot or Cyrus support common mail storage formats like Maildir or mbox, but organizations can configure servers to work with custom database-backed storage systems or integrate with distributed file systems depending on scalability or redundancy requirements. For example, enterprises managing large-scale email systems might choose to deploy IMAP servers connected to high-availability clustered file systems or cloud storage backends to ensure data durability and optimized access performance across geographic locations.

Customizing authentication mechanisms is another crucial aspect of IMAP deployment. While IMAP supports traditional authentication methods like plaintext passwords and CRAM-MD5, many organizations require integration with centralized identity management platforms. IMAP servers can be configured to authenticate users against LDAP directories, Active Directory domains, or OAuth2-based identity providers. Advanced customizations may include the integration of single sign-on (SSO) systems, enabling users to log in to their email accounts using the same credentials they use for other corporate applications. Some organizations may even develop custom authentication plugins to meet specific security or compliance requirements, such as integrating multifactor authentication or enforcing geofencing policies based on user location.

Customization also extends to access control and folder management within IMAP servers. Enterprises may need to implement granular permission models to restrict access to specific mailboxes, folders, or shared resources. IMAP servers can be configured to support Access Control Lists (ACLs), defining who can read, write, delete, or manage folders within shared mailboxes. For example, in a customer support environment, a shared mailbox might be configured to allow support agents to read and respond to incoming emails but restrict the ability to delete messages or change folder structures to team leads or administrators. These permissions can be enforced at the server level to ensure consistency and prevent unauthorized actions across all IMAP clients.

Another area where IMAP customization is frequently applied is in optimizing performance and resource utilization. Enterprises operating large-scale IMAP infrastructures can tune server configurations to manage connection limits, adjust thread pools, and implement caching strategies based on specific usage patterns. Some organizations may develop custom load-balancing mechanisms that direct IMAP traffic based on user roles, geographic locations, or server health metrics. By deploying IMAP servers behind smart load balancers or reverse proxies, administrators can ensure high availability and efficient distribution of workload across multiple server nodes.

Custom scripting and automation are often used to extend IMAP server functionality. Many IMAP servers provide hooks or plugin architectures that allow administrators to execute custom scripts in response to specific events, such as when a message is received, a folder is created, or a user logs in. These scripts can automate a variety of tasks, such as triggering antivirus scans, forwarding messages to external systems, applying custom labels, or initiating archival processes. For instance, an organization might implement a script that automatically moves incoming invoices to a specific folder and notifies the finance department via an integration with a messaging platform like Slack or Microsoft Teams.

Integration with other enterprise systems is another compelling reason for customizing IMAP deployments. Modern organizations often require IMAP servers to interoperate with customer relationship management (CRM) systems, enterprise resource planning (ERP) platforms, and document management solutions. Custom API connectors or middleware can be developed to allow IMAP servers to send and receive data from these external systems. For example, sales teams might benefit from an IMAP integration that automatically logs customer correspondence into a CRM platform, ensuring that all interactions are tracked and easily accessible from within the CRM interface.

In environments with specific compliance requirements, customization also includes implementing advanced logging and auditing capabilities. IMAP servers can be configured to generate detailed logs that capture user activities, such as message access, modifications, and deletions, as well as administrative actions like mailbox provisioning or policy changes. These logs may be integrated with Security Information and Event Management (SIEM) systems to enable real-time monitoring and alerting. Some organizations take customization further by developing bespoke reporting tools that extract insights from IMAP logs, helping them meet audit requirements for data protection regulations such as GDPR or HIPAA.

On the client side, IMAP customization enhances the user experience and ensures that email workflows align with organizational processes. Email clients can be configured with custom templates, folder structures, and synchronization rules. For instance, organizations may preconfigure email clients to include predefined folders for projects, teams, or departments, promoting consistency in how users organize their mailboxes. Custom plugins or extensions for IMAP clients can also automate repetitive tasks, such as message tagging, priority setting, or integration with task management applications.

Custom IMAP deployments also allow for tailored security configurations. Administrators may enforce policies that require all IMAP connections to use strong encryption protocols, restrict access based on IP whitelisting, or implement client certificate-based authentication. In sensitive environments, organizations may deploy IMAP servers within isolated network segments, using VPNs or private network peering to limit exposure to external threats.

Customizing IMAP deployments is not limited to large enterprises. Small and medium-sized businesses also leverage customization to create email systems that address their unique operational needs. Open-source IMAP servers, such as Dovecot, Cyrus, and Courier, are particularly popular in this context due to their modularity and extensibility. By tailoring configurations to match organizational workflows, businesses can maximize efficiency, improve security, and reduce costs associated with third-party email services.

Ultimately, the ability to customize IMAP deployments provides organizations with a versatile toolkit for building email infrastructures that are secure, scalable, and aligned with their business objectives. By fine-tuning every aspect of the IMAP environment—from storage backends and authentication methods to workflow automation and client configurations—organizations can create a tailored email experience that enhances productivity and supports long-term operational success.

Best Practices in IMAP Management

Effective IMAP management is essential for ensuring secure, efficient, and reliable email services within any organization. As a widely adopted protocol for remote email access and synchronization, IMAP underpins the majority of modern email infrastructures, providing centralized control over user mailboxes while enabling users to interact with their emails from multiple devices and locations. To ensure optimal performance and security, administrators must follow a set of best practices that cover server configuration, security hardening, resource optimization, and user experience considerations.

One of the foundational best practices in IMAP management is enforcing strong encryption for all IMAP traffic. IMAP servers must be configured to require TLS for all client-server communications to protect sensitive data such as login credentials and email contents from interception during transit. Administrators should disable plaintext connections on port 143 or enforce the mandatory use of STARTTLS. Furthermore, the IMAP server's TLS configuration should be regularly audited to ensure the use of modern cipher suites and protocols, while older and less secure protocols such as SSLv3 and weak ciphers should be disabled. Deploying certificates from trusted certificate authorities and maintaining regular renewal schedules helps avoid service disruptions and enhances trustworthiness.

Another critical best practice is the implementation of secure and scalable authentication mechanisms. IMAP servers should be integrated with centralized identity providers such as LDAP, Active Directory, or SAML-based systems to enforce uniform access control policies. Modern environments are encouraged to adopt OAuth2-based authentication workflows, which leverage token-based access to minimize password exposure and support multifactor authentication (MFA). For environments still using traditional username and password logins, administrators should enforce strong password policies and implement account lockout mechanisms to mitigate the risk of brute-force attacks.

Resource optimization plays a vital role in maintaining a responsive IMAP infrastructure. Administrators should configure connection limits, thread pools, and memory usage parameters based on the expected user load and hardware capabilities. Load balancers can be introduced to distribute client connections evenly across multiple IMAP server nodes, enhancing system resilience and scalability. In large-scale deployments, server clustering and shared storage architectures, such as network-attached storage or distributed file systems, ensure high availability and efficient handling of large mailbox sizes. Caching mechanisms, including mailbox index caching and metadata caching, can further enhance performance by reducing the number of direct disk I/O operations required to process user requests.

Mailbox management best practices recommend regular maintenance of mailbox data to prevent performance degradation. Organizations should implement policies that automatically archive older emails to secondary storage or archive servers, keeping active mailboxes lean and improving synchronization times for IMAP clients. Tools and scripts can be used to automate the archiving of messages older than a specified date or above certain mailbox size thresholds. Encouraging users to organize their emails using folders and subfolders helps prevent inbox bloat and ensures that message retrieval and synchronization remain efficient.

Security monitoring is a cornerstone of IMAP management. Administrators should implement detailed logging of all IMAP server activities, including login attempts, mailbox access, and administrative actions. These logs must be regularly reviewed or integrated with centralized Security Information and Event Management (SIEM) platforms to identify anomalies and potential security incidents. Automated intrusion detection and prevention systems (IDPS) can be used to monitor IMAP logs for patterns indicative of malicious activity, such as repeated failed login attempts or unusual access times, and take proactive measures such as IP blocking or user account lockdowns.

Data backup and disaster recovery planning are essential components of IMAP management. Regular, automated backups of mailbox data ensure that email communications can be restored in the event of data loss, hardware failures, or cyber incidents such as ransomware attacks. Backup strategies should include both full and incremental backups and ensure that stored backups are encrypted and replicated to offsite or cloud storage locations. Periodic testing of backup and recovery procedures is necessary to validate that the process functions as expected and that service recovery objectives can be met during real incidents.

User experience should also be prioritized within IMAP management. Administrators should configure IMAP servers to support commonly used extensions such as IDLE for push notifications, CONDSTORE for efficient folder synchronization, and QRESYNC for incremental resynchronization. These extensions significantly enhance the responsiveness of IMAP clients, particularly in mobile and bandwidth-constrained environments. Support for advanced folder hierarchies, customizable namespaces, and mailbox quotas helps ensure that IMAP services can be tailored to meet diverse user needs.

Policy enforcement is another important aspect of IMAP management. Administrators should establish and document acceptable use policies that outline how employees should manage their mailboxes, including recommendations on message retention, mailbox organization, and secure email handling practices. Security awareness training helps users recognize phishing attempts, use secure passwords, and report suspicious activities, creating a culture of vigilance that complements technical security controls.

Integration with other enterprise services is an increasingly common best practice. IMAP servers should work in tandem with SMTP servers, antispam filters, antivirus engines, and data loss prevention (DLP) systems to provide comprehensive email protection. By integrating IMAP with compliance monitoring tools, organizations can automatically enforce data retention rules, message encryption policies, and access control requirements mandated by regulations such as GDPR, HIPAA, or SOX.

Regular patching and updates are necessary to mitigate vulnerabilities in IMAP software. Administrators should maintain an up-to-date inventory of IMAP server versions and promptly apply security patches as they are released by software vendors or open-source communities. Change management procedures should be in place to ensure that updates are tested in staging environments before being deployed to production servers, reducing the risk of service disruption caused by unanticipated software conflicts or bugs.

Finally, effective IMAP management requires continuous performance monitoring and capacity planning. Metrics such as CPU load, memory utilization, disk I/O, active connection counts, and mailbox growth rates should be collected and reviewed regularly to identify trends and predict future resource needs. By proactively scaling infrastructure or optimizing configurations based on these insights, administrators can maintain service quality as user demands evolve.

Following these best practices in IMAP management ensures that organizations deliver secure, reliable, and high-performing email services. By addressing security, performance, usability, and compliance, administrators can create a robust IMAP environment that supports both operational efficiency and long-term business objectives.

Case Studies in IMAP Modernization

IMAP modernization initiatives have been undertaken by numerous organizations seeking to enhance the scalability, security, and efficiency of their email infrastructures. These projects often address legacy systems that can no longer meet the demands of contemporary business operations. Through a series of case studies, it becomes clear that IMAP modernization is not only about upgrading technology but also about aligning email services with organizational growth, evolving user needs, and changing security landscapes.

One notable case involved a multinational financial services company with a legacy IMAP deployment that had been in place for over a decade. The organization faced significant performance issues due to outdated hardware, an absence of load balancing, and inefficient mailbox storage practices. Mailboxes exceeding tens of gigabytes were common, leading to sluggish synchronization and frustrated employees. To address these challenges, the company launched a modernization project focused on re-architecting its IMAP environment. By transitioning from aging physical servers to a containerized IMAP solution running on Kubernetes, the company achieved dynamic scaling capabilities, allowing IMAP servers to automatically adjust to fluctuating workloads. The deployment of a shared distributed storage system further improved read/write performance for mailbox data. As part of the modernization, administrators implemented IMAP extensions like QRESYNC and CONDSTORE to accelerate client synchronization, particularly for mobile devices. The outcome was a 40% reduction in email-related support tickets and a measurable increase in employee productivity, as synchronization times dropped from minutes to mere seconds.

Another example comes from a government agency that was operating a secure IMAP system but struggling to meet modern compliance requirements, including strict data sovereignty and auditing mandates. The legacy environment lacked encryption by default, and user credentials were still being transmitted using outdated authentication methods such as plaintext login. The agency embarked on a full modernization of its IMAP services, which included integrating the IMAP servers with the national identity provider for federated authentication and enforcing TLS encryption across all communications. The IMAP servers were reconfigured to support OAuth2, enabling multifactor authentication for employees accessing their mailboxes both onsite and remotely. To address data sovereignty concerns, the agency migrated its IMAP infrastructure to a private cloud hosted in a government-owned data center. The modernization effort also introduced an integrated logging system that fed IMAP logs into a centralized SIEM platform, ensuring compliance with security auditing standards. Following the project, the agency achieved full regulatory compliance, significantly reduced the attack surface of its email environment, and gained real-time visibility into all IMAP-related activities.

In the healthcare sector, a hospital network faced growing concerns over email system reliability and data protection. The existing IMAP servers were hosted on legacy infrastructure that could not meet the high availability and redundancy standards required for healthcare operations. Downtime incidents were frequent, often disrupting the communication of critical patient information. The modernization strategy involved replacing the legacy servers with a cluster of IMAP servers deployed in a high-availability configuration across two geographically redundant data centers. Load balancers were introduced to distribute traffic and ensure failover capabilities in case of hardware or network failures. Additionally, end-to-end encryption was enforced, with the deployment of S/MIME for message-level encryption on top of IMAP's transport-layer security. Automated backup solutions were integrated into the new architecture, providing daily snapshots of all mailboxes that were replicated to a secure, offsite location. As a result, the hospital network eliminated unplanned outages, ensured compliance with HIPAA data protection rules, and restored user confidence in the reliability of their email communications.

An educational institution consisting of multiple campuses also embarked on a major IMAP modernization effort. The university had grown rapidly, leading to an overloaded and fragmented email system with multiple isolated IMAP servers across different faculties. The lack of centralization made mailbox management cumbersome for IT staff and complicated user migrations between campuses. To resolve this, the university implemented a centralized IMAP platform hosted in a private cloud. The modernization project consolidated all user mailboxes onto a unified IMAP infrastructure that included directory synchronization with the university's Active Directory system. Students and faculty could now access their mailboxes from a single authentication domain, simplifying account management and reducing administrative overhead. The deployment of the IMAP IDLE extension further enhanced real-time message delivery for thousands of mobile and desktop clients. This modernization initiative also paved the way for seamless integration with collaborative platforms such as Microsoft Teams and Moodle, bridging the gap between email and learning management systems. User satisfaction surveys conducted post-modernization indicated a marked improvement in perceived email performance and accessibility across all campuses.

A large e-commerce company modernized its IMAP services as part of a broader digital transformation strategy aimed at improving customer support operations. The company's legacy IMAP system struggled with delays in message delivery and limited integration with customer support tools. The modernization effort focused on integrating the IMAP servers with the company's CRM and ticketing system. Automated workflows were developed to extract customer inquiries from incoming emails, populate CRM records, and trigger ticket generation without manual intervention. Custom IMAP filters were created to categorize incoming emails by region, product line, and issue severity, allowing the support team to prioritize responses more effectively. The IMAP environment was also reconfigured to handle a significant increase in email traffic driven by seasonal sales spikes. By modernizing its IMAP deployment and automating routine tasks, the e-commerce company reduced average ticket response times by 30%, improved customer satisfaction ratings, and increased the efficiency of its support staff.

These case studies illustrate how IMAP modernization is more than just a technical upgrade; it is a strategic initiative that transforms how organizations manage email services. Whether driven by the need to enhance performance, comply with regulatory frameworks, improve system reliability, or streamline workflows, modernizing IMAP infrastructure creates long-lasting benefits that extend to both end users and IT teams. Each example demonstrates that with proper planning and execution, IMAP can continue to serve as a flexible and dependable backbone for email communication in even the most demanding and evolving environments.

Conclusion and Next Steps

IMAP has long served as a foundational protocol in the world of email management, and as organizations continue to evolve their IT strategies, IMAP remains a critical component of secure, scalable, and efficient communication infrastructures. The modernization of IMAP environments is no longer simply an option but a necessity for businesses navigating increasingly complex digital ecosystems. Through the implementation of advanced security practices, integration with cloud and hybrid environments, automation, and the incorporation of modern extensions and protocols, organizations can significantly enhance the performance and resilience of their email systems. The chapters discussed throughout this book have demonstrated that while IMAP is rooted in decades-old technology, it is anything but obsolete. Instead, it continues to adapt to the demands of modern enterprises.

Moving forward, organizations that rely on IMAP must approach email management as part of a broader, holistic IT strategy. Email systems are not isolated applications; they intersect with collaboration platforms, regulatory compliance requirements, customer relationship management systems, and cybersecurity initiatives. Therefore, IMAP modernization should be executed with cross-functional collaboration between IT teams, security experts, compliance officers, and business stakeholders. This ensures that the modernization efforts address not only technical challenges but also business goals such as operational efficiency, user productivity, and regulatory adherence.

Security will remain a top priority in the ongoing evolution of IMAP deployments. The rise in cyberattacks targeting email infrastructures has underscored the importance of enforcing end-to-end encryption, implementing multi-factor authentication, and monitoring IMAP environments continuously for anomalies. While TLS is now a widely adopted standard, the growing threat landscape demands constant vigilance, patch management, and the integration of advanced monitoring and response systems. Security must be viewed not as a one-time effort but as a continuous process of assessment, improvement, and adaptation to emerging threats.

Automation will also play a significant role in shaping the future of IMAP management. As organizations seek to reduce the burden on IT teams and improve service delivery, automation tools that leverage IMAP APIs and integrate with workflow platforms will become increasingly indispensable. Automating common tasks such as email sorting, ticket creation, data extraction, and compliance auditing can deliver immediate operational benefits. The ability to integrate IMAP with AI-powered tools will further streamline processes, enabling predictive email management, intelligent categorization, and the automatic triggering of business processes based on email content and context.

Cloud adoption will continue to influence the way IMAP is deployed and managed. Organizations that once relied solely on on-premises infrastructures are now embracing hybrid or fully cloud-based environments. IMAP servers can be effectively containerized and deployed within cloud-native frameworks, allowing for more flexible scaling, resource optimization, and high availability across multiple regions. Modern IMAP deployments will increasingly leverage container orchestration platforms like Kubernetes to automate scaling and resource allocation, ensuring that email services remain responsive and reliable even during periods of high demand.

Another emerging area is the deepening integration between IMAP and collaboration ecosystems. As communication shifts away from siloed email-only workflows toward interconnected platforms that blend messaging, file sharing, and task management, IMAP systems must adapt to coexist and integrate with these tools. Email clients and servers will increasingly provide built-in connectors or APIs that integrate with collaboration suites such as Microsoft Teams, Slack, and Google Workspace. The goal will be to present users with unified communication environments where email, chat, tasks, and project management coexist seamlessly, thereby reducing context switching and improving productivity.

Compliance and governance will also play a growing role in how IMAP systems are managed. As data privacy regulations continue to evolve globally, organizations will need to ensure that their IMAP implementations support features like data retention policies, message encryption at rest and in transit, and granular access controls. Integrating IMAP with compliance management tools and audit systems will allow administrators to generate reports, monitor adherence to internal policies, and respond to regulatory inquiries efficiently.

To effectively navigate these changes, IT teams must invest in continuous education and skills development. The modernization of IMAP requires expertise in not only email protocols but also in areas such as security engineering, cloud infrastructure, containerization, scripting, and automation frameworks. Fostering a culture of learning and adaptability within IT departments will position organizations to meet the evolving demands of IMAP management and broader email infrastructure challenges.

In parallel, organizations should embrace a proactive approach to capacity planning and performance optimization. As email volumes continue to rise and user expectations for instantaneous access grow, IMAP servers must be regularly evaluated and optimized. This includes monitoring system performance metrics, ensuring sufficient hardware and storage resources, and leveraging advanced synchronization extensions such as QRESYNC or CONDSTORE. Fine-tuning resource configurations, leveraging distributed storage systems, and implementing intelligent caching mechanisms will be essential to maintaining a high-performing email environment.

Lastly, communication between technical teams and end users should be a key component of any modernization strategy. User feedback is invaluable in identifying pain points within email workflows, and this input should be used to refine IMAP client configurations, improve folder structures, and ensure that synchronization settings align with real-world usage patterns. Providing users with training on best practices for managing their mailboxes, recognizing phishing attempts, and using email clients effectively will further enhance the impact of backend improvements.

The next steps for organizations will involve assessing the current state of their IMAP infrastructure, identifying areas of improvement, and developing a roadmap for modernization. Whether the focus is on improving performance, enhancing security, integrating with cloud and collaboration platforms, or automating operational tasks, the modernization of IMAP is an ongoing journey that delivers lasting benefits. By taking a strategic approach and leveraging the technologies and practices discussed throughout this book, organizations can position themselves for success in managing email as a vital and evolving component of their digital landscape.